Google SketchUp for Game Design
Beginner's Guide

Create 3D game worlds complete with textures,
levels, and props

Robin de Jongh

BIRMINGHAM - MUMBAI

Google SketchUp for Game Design
Beginner's Guide

First published: November 2011

Production Reference: 1181111

Published by Packt Publishing Ltd.
Livery Place
35 Livery Street
Birmingham B3 2PB, UK.

ISBN 978-1-84969-134-5

www.packtpub.com

Cover Image by Robin de Jongh (robin@sketchupuser.com)

Credits

Author
Robin de Jongh

Reviewers
Colin Holgate

Thomas Bleicher

Acquisition Editors
David Barnes

Wilson D'Souza

Development Editor
Hyacintha D'Souza

Technical Editor
Mohd. Sahil

Project Coordinator
Kushal Bhardwaj

Proofreader
Josh Toth

Indexer
Tejal Daruwale

Production Coordinator
Prachali Bhiwandkar

Cover Work
Prachali Bhiwandkar

About the Author

Robin de Jongh worked for many years as a Design Engineer and 3D modeler, where he became an early advocate of SketchUp. He has a degree in Computer-Aided Product Design from Nottingham Trent University, and is the author of *SketchUp for Architectural Visualization*: *Beginner's Guide*. He lives in England where he works as an editor of computer software and video games' books.

I would like to thank my wonderful wife for all her support. Thanks to my technical reviewers and everyone at Packt who has worked hard to make this book a success.

About the Reviewers

Colin Holgate has been programming for 30 years, using a variety of multimedia authoring tools, including HyperCard, LiveCode, Adobe Director, Adobe Flash, and Unity 3D. He has been a SketchUp Pro user since 2004, and has used SketchUp alongside Unity 3D to make a virtual walkthrough of the new World Trade Center site. The walkthrough is located at http://www.wtctwo.com/.

Colin was one of the two reviewers for the Packt book, *SketchUp 7.1 for Architectural Visualization*. Thomas Bleicher was the other reviewer.

Thomas Bleicher is a trained architect with a soft spot for daylight and computer simulation. He has worked as an architect and consultant in Germany and UK. In his spare time, he develops software for SketchUp and daylight analysis.

Currently, he lives in the Cayman Islands.

www.PacktPub.com

Support files, eBooks, discount offers, and more

You might want to visit www.PacktPub.com for support files and downloads related to your book.

Did you know that Packt offers eBook versions of every book published, with PDF and ePub files available? You can upgrade to the eBook version at www.PacktPub.com and as a print book customer, you are entitled to a discount on the eBook copy. Get in touch with us at service@packtpub.com for more details.

At www.PacktPub.com, you can also read a collection of free technical articles, sign up for a range of free newsletters and receive exclusive discounts and offers on Packt books and eBooks.

http://PacktLib.PacktPub.com

Do you need instant solutions to your IT questions? PacktLib is Packt's online digital book library. Here, you can access, read and search across Packt's entire library of books.

Why Subscribe?

- Fully-searchable across every book published by Packt
- Copy and paste, print and bookmark content
- On demand and accessible via web browser

Free Access for Packt account holders

If you have an account with Packt at www.PacktPub.com, you can use this to access PacktLib today and view nine entirely free books. Simply use your login credentials for immediate access.

Table of Contents

Preface   **1**

Chapter 1: Why Use SketchUp?   **7**

Commitment brings rewards   8

Is this book for me?   8

Can I really become a professional in the game and film industry?   9

What's SketchUp really good at?   9

How will this book help?   9

Some limitations   10

Making bags of cash-selling assets   11

The envy of the gaming community: creating custom levels   13

In-game level design tools   14

Modding assets   14

What have I learned?   14

Chapter 2: Tools that Grow on Trees   **15**

3D Warehouse   15

Time for action – research what's hot and what's not   16

Your best CG textures source   20

Signing up to CGTextures.com   21

Copyright issues with textures   23

Your library   23

Meshlab   24

Time for action – learning about 3D meshes in MeshLab   25

Moving around in 3D   27

File formats   28

Get your game engine here: Unity 3D   28

The pro games environment   29

Time for action – obtaining Unity 3D for free   29
Google SketchUp   34
  Enhanced texture packs   34
GIMP: The free professional graphics editor   36
Summary   37

Chapter 3: Wooden Pallet: Texture Creation   **39**
Finding textures to use in asset modeling   39
Time for action – selecting the photo texture   39
Enhancing textures   42
Time for action – cropping and enhancing   42
What are pixels?   45
  Texture sizes   46
Time for action – arranging multiple textures   47
Saving textures   51
  Naming conventions   52
  Copyright text   52
Time for action – final touches   52
Summary   54

Chapter 4: Wooden Pallet: Modeling   **55**
Your first model in SketchUp   56
Time for action – importing a texture to scale   57
  Modeling from the texture   58
Time for action – basic 3D geometry   58
Time for action – Push/Pull, Move, and Copy   62
  It's really that easy!   65
Time for action – multiple copies   65
The power of pre-prepared textures   67
Time for action – completing texturing   68
Time for action – recycling textures for use on non-vital faces   72
Preparing for game use   75
  Hidden geometry and layers   75
  Removing unseen faces   75
  Exploding geometry   77
  Purging unused geometry and materials   77
  Checking the face orientation   78
  Compressing and resizing textures   78
  Saving for game use   79
Summary   **79**

Chapter 5: Game Levels in SketchUp   81

Sketching out the level   83
Do game artists need art degrees?   83
Time for action – setting up the terrain grid and plan   86
Time for action – setting up the terrain texture image   89
Time for action – creating a color selection layer   92
The master texture   94
Time for action – creating a large seamless texture   95
Time for action – creating a tiled texture   98
Time for action – filling selected areas with textures   100
Time for action – using tileable textures from the Internet   102
Have a go hero – selecting and texturing   102
    Some nifty texture tweaks   103
Time for action – creating a roadside kerb   103
Time for action – removing white edges   105
    Modeling terrain with Sandbox tools   107
Time for action – adding height to a flat terrain   107
    The Stamp tool   110
Time for action – stamping detail onto the terrain   111
    The Drape tool   115
Time for action – using the Drape tool   116
    Uniting terrain geometry with texture   116
Summary   118

Chapter 6: Importing to a Professional Game Application: Unity 3D   119

Exporting the level from SketchUp   120
Time for action – preparing a model for export   120
Time for action – SketchUp Pro export   121
Time for action – SketchUp free export   122
Time for action – using the free Autodesk FBX converter   122
Importing to Unity 3D   123
Time for action – importing your terrain in to Unity   124
Time for action – using a high-resolution terrain texture in Unity   127
Creating lights   128
Time for action – creating Sunlight in Unity   129
Setting up your character controller   132
Time for action – setting up a first-person shooter style controller   132
Time for action – playing the level   133
Time for action – creating a web playable walkthrough   134
Time for action – copying and pasting the pallet multiple times   137
Summary   140

Chapter 7: Quick Standard Assets   **141**
  Rough and ready fencing   **142**
  Time for action – making fencing with SketchUp's materials   **142**
  Time for action – making several unique variations   **145**
  Inserting multiple copies to quickly fill out a level   **147**
  Time for action – fencing large areas   **148**
  Time for action – walking around in SketchUp to visualize your level   **151**
  Generating buildings quickly   **153**
  Time for action – creating a building from two images   **153**
  When the going gets tough   **157**
    Using someone else's assets   158
  Time for action – cleaning up a Google Warehouse model   **159**
    Fixing the origin and removing hidden geometry   160
    Rectifying scale issues   161
    Checking face alignment and textures   162
  The ten-minute oil barrel   **163**
  Creating tools or weapons   **166**
  Time for action – modeling a low polygon wrench   **166**
  Summary   **172**
Chapter 8: Advanced Modeling: Create a Realistic Car in Easy Steps   **173**
  Where to find car images and plans   **174**
  Time for action – creating a car texture   **174**
  Time for action – creating a 3D car outline   **178**
  Refining the car's geometry   **181**
  Time for action – sitting on the hood   **181**
  Modeling by hand   **187**
  Time for action – applying a car body filler with the pencil tool   **187**
  Creating the car texture from photos   **190**
    Finding car images   191
      Some websites with car textures   191
      Taking your own car images   191
      Find a friend in the trade   192
  Time for action   **192**
  Painting in individual elements   **196**
  Time for action – painting over the rear view   **196**
  Time for action – creating blend areas   **199**
    UV unwrap plugins   202
  Time for action – how realistic wheels make all the difference   **204**
  Summary   **205**

Chapter 9: The Main Building - Inside and Out   207

Creating the main building   208
Time for action – clipping round textures   208
Modeling the interior   215
Your final 3D game level in Unity 3D   217
Time for action – setting up a playable game level layout   218
Level-led design   223
Time for action – digging out a terrain   223
Time for action – exporting buildings to Unity 3D   227
Creating context with skyline and background terrain   229
Time for action – creating see-through textures   229
Time for action – creating a backdrop   231
Time for action – enabling see-through materials (Alpha Channel)   233
Time for action – enabling a skybox   234
Time for action – ambient light   236
Exporting your game for others to play   237
Time for action – who said you can't have your game and play it?   238
Summary   240

Appendix A: MakeHuman   241

Time for action – making a human   241

Appendix B: Pop Quiz Answers   247

Chapter 1: Why Use SketchUp   247
Chapter 2: Tools that Grow on Trees   247
Chapter 6: Importing to a Professional Game Application: Unity 3D   248

Index   249

Preface

Creating video game environments similar to the best 3D games in the market is now within the reach of hobbyists for the first time, with free availability of game development software such as Unity 3D, added to the ease with which groups of enthusiasts can get together to pool their skills for a game project. The sheer number of these independent game projects springing up means that there is a constant need for game art, physical 3D environments, and the objects that inhabit these game worlds. Thanks to Google there is an easy, fun way to create professional game art, levels, and props.

Google SketchUp is a natural choice for beginners for game designing. This book provides you with the workflow to build realistic 3D environments, levels, and props to fill your game world quickly. In simple steps, you will model terrains, buildings, vehicles, and much more.

Google SketchUp is an ideal entry-level modeling tool for game design, allowing you to take digital photographs and turn them into 3D objects for quick and fun game creation. SketchUp for Game Design takes you through the modeling of a game level with SketchUp and Unity 3D, complete with all game art, textures, and props. You will learn how to create cars, buildings, terrain, tools, and standard level props, such as barrels, fencing, and wooden pallets. You will set up your game level in Unity 3D to create a fully functional first-person walk-around level to e-mail your friends or future employers.

When you have completed the projects in this book, you will be comfortable creating 3D worlds, be it for games, visualization, or films.

What this book covers

Chapter 1, *Why Use SketchUp?*, is our introduction to Google SketchUp as an indispensable game development tool. Google SketchUp is the ideal entry-level game design tool for rapid generation of levels and props. This chapter gives an introduction to SketchUp and tells us why it's the easiest, most dependable software for rapidly creating levels and props for your 3D games.

Chapter 2, Tools that Grow on Trees, describes the tools that you need to create your own AAA game creation studio—and it's entirely free! We also do some research into what game assets sell the most, and where you can find online stores to make some money yourself.

Chapter 3, Wooden Pallet: Texture Creation, tells us how to create a realistic game texture from a photo, using GIMP, the free fully-featured image editing studio.

Chapter 4, Wooden Pallet: Simple Texturing Techniques, details about the most useful SketchUp toolset by creating a high-detail, low-polygon game prop.

Chapter 5, Game Levels in SketchUp, allows you to create a game level complete with terrain, realistic textures, and shadows using SketchUp's amazing Sandbox sculpting tools.

Chapter 6, Import to a Professional Game Application: Unity 3D, allows you to create a game level complete with terrain, realistic textures, and shadows using SketchUp's amazing Sandbox sculpting tools.

Chapter 7, Quick Standard Assets, helps you create a rusty fence, a barrel, a wrench, some quick buildings, and more, using SketchUp tools.

Chapter 8, Advanced Modeling: Create a Realistic Car in Easy Steps, describes the amazing modeling capabilities of SketchUp for game design. It also allows you to create a game level complete with terrain, realistic textures, and shadows using SketchUp's amazing Sandbox sculpting tools.

Chapter 9, The Main Building - Inside and Out, brings together all your skills into a single game, setting up the game environment including a backdrop, sky, and fog. You will create your detailed main building complete with maze-like interior and export an executable fully-playable game to send to your friends or to show off on the Web.

Appendix A, MakeHuman, makes use of the MakeHuman software to create a textured, high-polygon human model, and then shows you how to use MeshLab to reduce polygons.

What you need for this book

All you need is a PC or Mac with an Internet connection. A 3-button mouse with a scroll wheel is also beneficial.

Who this book is for

This book is designed for anyone who wants to create the entire 3D worlds into use in freely available game engines such as Unity 3D, CryEngine, Ogre, Panda3D, Unreal Engine, or Blender Game Engine. The book is also for all those of you who wish to create new levels and assets to sell in-game asset stores or to use in visualization or animation.

Conventions

In this book, you will find several headings appearing frequently.

To give clear instructions of how to complete a procedure or task, we use:

Time for action – heading

1. Action 1

2. Action 2

3. Action 3

Instructions often need some extra explanation so that they make sense, so they are followed with:

What just happened?

This heading explains the working of tasks or instructions that you have just completed.

You will also find some other learning aids in the book, including:

Pop quiz – heading

These are short multiple choice questions intended to help you test your own understanding.

Have a go hero – heading

These set practical challenges and give you ideas for experimenting with what you have learned.

You will also find a number of styles of text that distinguish between different kinds of information. Here are some examples of these styles, and an explanation of their meaning.

Code words in text are shown as follows: "Save the image as a PNG file named `Map_Selection.png`."

New terms and **important words** are shown in bold. Words that you see on the screen, in menus or dialog boxes for example, appear in the text like this: "Go to **Members ¦ Login** and use your new username and password to log in to the website."

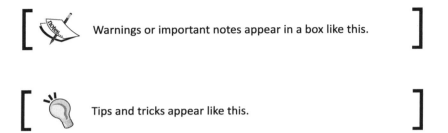

Warnings or important notes appear in a box like this.

Tips and tricks appear like this.

Reader feedback

Feedback from our readers is always welcome. Let us know what you think about this book—what you liked or may have disliked. Reader feedback is important for us to develop titles that you really get the most out of.

To send us general feedback, simply send an e-mail to feedback@packtpub.com, and mention the book title via the subject of your message.

If there is a book that you need and would like to see us publish, please send us a note in the **SUGGEST A TITLE** form on www.packtpub.com or e-mail suggest@packtpub.com.

If there is a topic that you have expertise in and you are interested in either writing or contributing to a book, see our author guide on www.packtpub.com/authors.

Customer support

Now that you are the proud owner of a Packt book, we have a number of things to help you to get the most from your purchase.

Downloading the color images of this book

We also provide you a PDF file that has color images of the screenshots used in this book. The high resolution color images will help you better understand the changes in the output. You can download this file from http://www.packtpub.com/sites/default/files/downloads/1345_sketchupimages

Errata

Although we have taken every care to ensure the accuracy of our content, mistakes do happen. If you find a mistake in one of our books—maybe a mistake in the text or the code—we would be grateful if you would report this to us. By doing so, you can save other readers from frustration and help us improve subsequent versions of this book. If you find any errata, please report them by visiting http://www.packtpub.com/support, selecting your book, clicking on the **errata submission form** link, and entering the details of your errata. Once your errata are verified, your submission will be accepted and the errata will be uploaded on our website, or added to any list of existing errata, under the Errata section of that title. Any existing errata can be viewed by selecting your title from http://www.packtpub.com/support.

Piracy

Piracy of copyright material on the Internet is an ongoing problem across all media. At Packt, we take the protection of our copyright and licenses very seriously. If you come across any illegal copies of our works, in any form, on the Internet, please provide us with the location address or website name immediately so that we can pursue a remedy.

Please contact us at copyright@packtpub.com with a link to the suspected pirated material.

We appreciate your help in protecting our authors, and our ability to bring you valuable content.

Questions

You can contact us at questions@packtpub.com if you are having a problem with any aspect of the book, and we will do our best to address it.

1
Why Use SketchUp?

Imagine you're in Los Angeles. You're sitting at a round table covered with expensive champagne and caviar. Brad Pitt and Angelina Jolie are sitting opposite you, and you've been getting on like old friends. That's natural—you spent four months with them last Summer. On stage, Kevin Spacey announces the winner of this year's Oscar for Best Director. It's you. As you stand and make your way to the podium you feel familiar nerves. You begin your acceptance speech, "This is really embarrassing for me as I'm not even a film director, and I'm really running out of things to say now—I've already been up here seven times. So, I'll tell you how this whole amazing journey started for me. It started with a book called SketchUp for Game Design."

You might think that the journey you're starting with this book will end with only some mods on your favorite game. Or you might expect, at the most, to sell some game assets on the Internet. You may not have bargained for this introduction. However, it is well within the realm of possibility. Last time you unwrapped and installed a new 3D game, you probably noticed the unbelievable realism that is now achieved in game design. This realism is due to the assets contained in the game, as well as the effects provided by the game engine. Due to the magnificent computational power hidden in just an average gaming computer, these assets are now approaching the same detail level of those used in film animation. In other words, CG film and game assets will no longer be any different.

When you have completed the projects in this book, you will be able to create 3D worlds— whether for games, visualization, or film. Your assets will be indistinguishable from real world artifacts. You will be documenting the world in 3D computer space. Given that it is said the future of film and gaming will ultimately bring the two together, you could find yourself becoming a master of both!

Commitment brings rewards

I want to talk to you from the outset about passion and commitment. If you commit to this book, it will commit to you. If you passionately apply what it tells you, in both the tutorials and principles discussed, you will find yourself on the road to stardom. It may be stardom in a small gaming company in your own neighborhood. It may be superstardom both in game and big screen. Still, passion and commitment are required for both these outcomes. The methods shown in this book are not hard to apply. Best of all, they do not require talent. The entry level for this profession is reachable, and you can make it. I would liken it to a brand new Olympic event running for the first year. There aren't many pros out there because the event is so new. Given that you train for the next four years you are almost guaranteed a place in your national team. Do you remember the film **Cool Runnings**? It's like that! Once you're in the team you will make what you can of it.

Creating assets for game and film is simply a matter of documenting the world around you. SketchUp gives you the tools to do that. You could spend ten or twenty times more than the price of SketchUp Pro and you wouldn't be any better off. In fact, you'd be worse off in the long run. Why? Because SketchUp users will create assets ten times faster than you can and, before you know it, you will have to start using SketchUp anyway. Here's a quote from a professional game designer who uses SketchUp. This is Ken Nguyen, a concept artist in the game and movie industries:

> *"I can build low and high detailed models (architecture and props) much faster than someone using for example Maya or Max. Moreover, if the game engine allows you to upload the models, one can see in a few minutes or hours if the models work or not, if the sizes are right instead of waiting a day or more for the models to be finished by a Maya/Max modeler."*

There it is from the horse's mouth. What are you waiting for?

Is this book for me?

If you work (or want to work) in any industry that uses 3D assets, this book is for you. If you are an enthusiast, it's for you, too. You can follow everything in here, either on a PC or Mac. You can do it completely for free with the free version of SketchUp and free file converters. Best of all, the game engines you'll be using are also free. See the next chapter for more details about **Unity 3D**. As well as these obvious industries, web designers are catching on, too. There will be a large market for asset designers for **Google Earth** now that you can explore inside a building as well as outside it. The potential for replicating every store, museum, and park within Google Earth is immense, and so is the possibility for advertising revenue. Will Google shift their entire search engine into 3D web space? What if it does?

Can I really become a professional in the game and film industry?

As you've already seen, there is enormous crossover between the two industries. In the future, there will be no difference between the 3D assets used in the film and the game spin-off. Gamers will walk around the same sets that were used in the film, simply because the film sets will be entirely digital assets. This also means that the bar for entry into the film industry is lowered significantly. If you are a skilful SketchUp asset creator, you will be able to create a set for a fraction of the cost of the real thing. This means as long as you can afford a couple of actors and a blue screen setup, you're well away to being an Indie Film Director. Okay, that's simplifying it too much. It may take a larger team than just you to create a full-length film, but there's no reason why you can't be a spoke in a bigger wheel, or even the hub itself.

What's SketchUp really good at?

There are a multitude of things that SketchUp is good at. In fact, there are a multitude of things SketchUp is world-class at, though there are only two things that it is so good at that there's no direct competition.

There's also two things that are easily the most important considerations when creating 3D assets.

Not surprisingly, these two things coincide with game asset design.

- Fast modeling of simple 3D geometry
- Fast texturing of simple 3D geometry

Leaving everything else aside, if you concentrate on these two you will win with asset creation. This is why you should use SketchUp, and why it is ludicrous to use Max or Maya which are designed to be used for all sorts of other things too. They're a jack of all trades, masters of none. SketchUp is a master of these two attributes, which are most necessary to asset creation.

How will this book help?

I've written this book honestly. I've kept my feet on the ground. That's what will help you where other books have failed you. I must confess that I've leafed through a lot of books on 3D modeling over the years and I have been absolutely disgusted with the dishonesty of those authors. I mean, you pick up a book with the promise on the cover that goes something like "Master complete figure modeling and rigging" backed up by a beautifully textured and rendered figure on the cover. When you get the book home and labor over it for a couple of hours, you realize that the only way of creating that figure on the cover is by loading the example files from the attached CD.

In most of these books, the tutorials are not realistic, which means that you, the reader, cannot replicate what's being offered. They have steps such as "continue editing vertices until your face takes shape." Hang on there! A face? A human face? There are seven billion human beings in the world all with subtly different faces so that we can recognize each one. Such is the level of detail in the face. You expect me to sculpt it in Zbrush with just a paragraph of explanation? Well yes, apparently!

The same goes for tutorials in magazines. I recently saw a tutorial on character modeling where the artist even claimed to have sculpted the finely muscled hero in four easy steps, when the model by all accounts appeared to be imported from Poser or Daz. Maybe I'm exaggerating just a little bit, but this kind of dishonesty really bugs me because, like you, I just want to learn the skills. I'd rather learn how to model an Aardvark really well than be promised a finely muscled human and end up with a blob that looks more like an anthill.

My promise to you as an author and someone who has had just as much frustration learning the skills as you have, is that I will only present the things I know you can, and will, model successfully. The upshot of this is that the front cover might not look as spangled and promising as the dishonest books. Neither will this book cover every single 3D modeling subject that each need a book by themselves, but it will provide a solid foundation to build on. I think that's a trade off that I know you're going to be fine with. In this book, we're interested in assets that will sell or make a difference in your games or movie sets.

 You can get the tutorial models and source textures for this book by going to http://www.packtpub.com and selecting this book title. Scroll down and click on **Code Bundle** and enter your e-mail address to receive the download link.

Some limitations

Because we're talking about being honest, I'll admit one or two things. While SketchUp is the best you can get by a long way, SketchUp is not perfect. There are currently some limitations with the way images map onto geometry that sometimes requires you to import to the other software to finish the job quicker. Such as when you are texturing a highly-detailed model and need to use texture unwrapping. Modeling is also frustrating when there's a hole in your geometry and you just can't get it to plug up! These are things that I hope you'll get used to over time and you'll find ways of working through them. I can't list fixes for them all here, so it's best just to remind you that the various SketchUp user forums are some of the most helpful on the Internet. Also, if you've bought a license of SketchUp Pro, don't forget it comes with free e-mail support.

Making bags of cash selling assets

Can I really make money selling assets created in SketchUp? Let's take a look. Here's a screenshot from the online asset store for Vue users at `http://www.cornucopia3d.com`. Vue is primarily used for outdoor virtual photography (rendering outdoor scenes) and so the Vue users are always in need of buildings and props.

Objects > **Roman Classical Triumphal Arch**
Brokered for Alain Bouchet et Eric Audibert

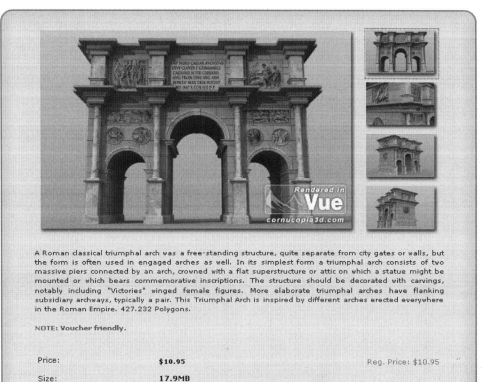

A Roman classical triumphal arch was a free-standing structure, quite separate from city gates or walls, but the form is often used in engaged arches as well. In its simplest form a triumphal arch consists of two massive piers connected by an arch, crowned with a flat superstructure or attic on which a statue might be mounted or which bears commemorative inscriptions. The structure should be decorated with carvings, notably including "Victories" winged female figures. More elaborate triumphal arches have flanking subsidiary archways, typically a pair. This Triumphal Arch is inspired by different arches erected everywhere in the Roman Empire. 427.232 Polygons.

NOTE: Voucher friendly.

Price:	**$10.95**	Reg. Price: $10.95
Size:	**17.9MB**	

There you have it, a beautifully detailed model of the triumphal arch in Rome, $10.95 and it's simply cannon fodder for SketchUp users. Now, that's at the cheap end of the market because Cornucopia is used mostly by hobbyists. Shown next is another model of the same monument, this time, at the professional end of the scale at http://www.Turbosquid.com.

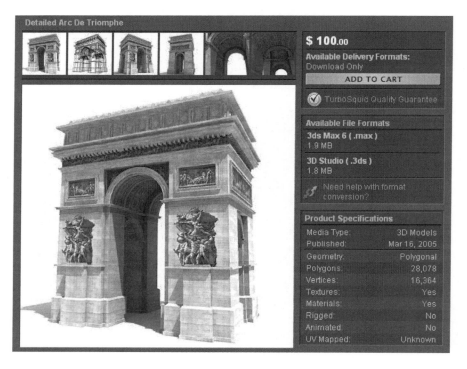

This one's up at $100 for each and every download. A lot of money for an asset, you might say? But if you scroll down you can see it's got 4 ratings from customers, proving it's bagged at least $400 for this asset creator, probably more. Now that's not bad for a few days' modeling, is it? The model has been up since 2005 but it hasn't cost the creator a penny to leave it there generating currency for his or her holiday fund.

Yes, you can sell your assets created in SketchUp, if you follow this book and put some effort into your work.

Pop quiz

Here's a really quick quiz to get you into the Beginner's Guide way of learning.

1. What are the two most important requirements for asset creation?

    a. High polygon counts and high-resolution texturing

    b. High-level modeling and rendering tools

    c. Fast modeling and fast texturing capabilities

2. Can I sell the assets I created with SketchUp online?

    a. No, the quality from SketchUp is too low

    b. Absolutely, as long as I take the learning experience seriously

    c. Yes, but I won't make much money

The envy of the gaming community: creating custom levels

People all over the world play games. They've been doing it for ages. People always long to play alongside other people, rather than on their own, and it's the same with computer games. Virtual gaming worlds have sprung up with immense success. Games where teams can work together or against human opponents, such as Second Life, World of Warcraft, Halo, games where teams can work together, or against human opponents. Gaming brings people together in virtual worlds who would never get to meet in person. Games cross the boundaries of language and culture. When you start to take part in a community like, this you start to gain approval. After a while this turns to kudos, then adoration, and a following can develop. In the end, you have your own fan base. I have seen this happen time and again for extra-helpful forum members, game level creators, or tutorial writers. This kind of kudos can be the biggest reward available, much more satisfying than financial rewards.

If thanks and kudos are what motivates you, you've come to the right place. With this book, you will be able to mod your favorite games. You will be able to create the new game levels and release them for free to the community. You will be able to churn out detailed and professional assets for your friends to use. Just remember one rule: Do it for free, and don't be needy in your pursuit of praise. If you're good and you're consistent, it will come.

In-game level design tools

Many games come bundled with a level or map editor. Some have gone so far as to release the whole game development kit with the game, and you might be able to use this with SketchUp as your asset modeling tool. Find a good example of this and stick with it for a while. Learn the ins and outs of the game and the editor. Use the skills you learn in this book to create new game levels or customize the existing ones. If you are able to show that your levels are downloaded and popular, this will be an excellent portfolio to use in approaching a game company. Furthermore, the feedback you get from those playing your levels (good and bad) will help you hone your skills like nothing else.

Modding assets

Even if your favorite game doesn't have a level editor bundled with it, you can still make an impact with your new asset creation skills. Texture maps on your computer are usually saved somewhere accessible to you, so at the least you can take these and modify them to your own preferences. I once took great delight in mapping a photo of my own face on my gaming character, then running around creating mayhem.

What have I learned?

In this chapter, you have learned a little about SketchUp and how it excels at game asset modeling:

- The two most outstanding features of SketchUp
- SketchUp's limitations for game asset modeling
- The convergence of gaming and film
- Introduction to selling assets
- How SketchUp is taking over from high-end applications like Maya and Max?
- Where to find additional help

In the next chapter, you will find out what software you need to make game level and asset creation a swift and easy process.

2
Tools that Grow on Trees

Did you ever dream as a kid that you'd stumble across a house made entirely of sweets and cake? You ate some of the door as you walked in, broke off bits of the table to shove in your bulging pockets, then you woke up and your wicked step mom told you that places like that didn't exist.

She was wrong! They do exist, and they are a lot bigger and better than you ever dreamt of as a child. Where is it? Down the phone line from your computer. It's the Internet. Just like the wicked witch in the story of Hansel and Gretel, the software companies that populate the Internet feel that giving away things for free is the only way to get customers to drop by. This actually encourages their competitors do the same, and in time the giveaways become bigger and better. A good example is Google SketchUp. Google decided that in order to increase the number of people worldwide creating 3D building assets for Google Earth, it would release the best asset creation software ever for free. Now the best marketing company ever is marketing the best asset modeling software ever and has linked it in to the biggest 3D environment ever which, by the way, it has also released for free. It's best to not overthink the possibilities, rather jump in and start using it. And that's what we'll do.

3D Warehouse

Google's **3D Warehouse** is the place where anyone can upload a 3D model for others to download. It's like **YouTube** for 3D assets. It's worth familiarizing yourself with the 3D Warehouse right at the start because you'll find it an integral part of your game-level creation process. After all, you don't need to make everything yourself, especially if there are bags of good examples already out there. Next, looking at what other people have done well (and badly) helps you to hone your skills. Finally, you need to get an idea of what's popular and what's not if you are to sell your assets, and 3D Warehouse is a good place to do that research because you can see a lot of usage statistics.

Time for action – research what's hot and what's not

1. Go to the Google 3D Warehouse at
    `http://sketchup.google.com/3dwarehouse/`.

2. Select **Advanced Search** as shown in this image:

3. You now have a whole host of search criteria you can use. Select the ones circled
    in the next screenshot.

4. Enter the asterisk symbol (*) in the top search box that says **Find items with
    all of these words in the title**.

5. Click on **Search**.

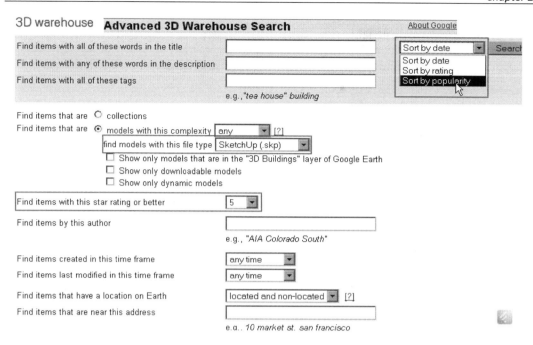

6. Make sure the **sort selection box** is set to **Sorted by popularity.**

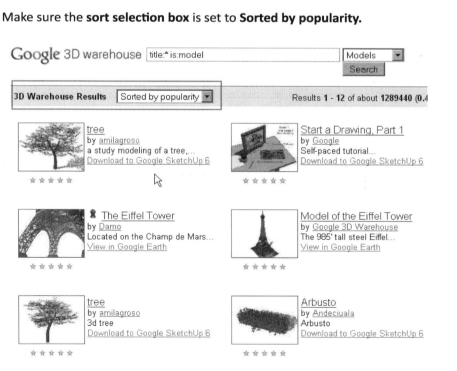

7. You now have a list of all the 5-star quality SketchUp models sorted by popularity. The most popular ones are the models that have been downloaded the most.

8. Scroll through these using the page navigation tool shown below and take a look at what's hot.

9. You can also do the same with unpopular (single-star) models, too.

10. Click on a model and use the **3D View** button to look around it.

11. You can tell how many views and downloads this model has had, as you can see marked in the previous screenshot.

12. Click on the graph icon.

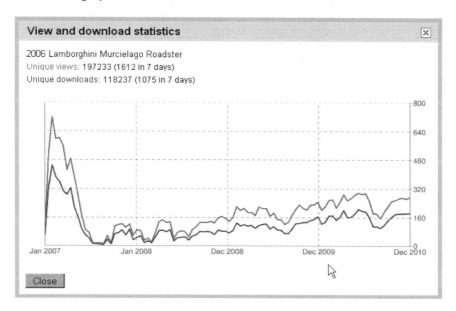

13. You can now see how many *views per day* this model has had. This is a phenomenal number, but only the most popular get this much attention. In *Chapter 9, The Main Building—Inside and Out,* you will learn how to model a car as good as this.

What just happened?

You used 3D Warehouse to start your asset research: what's popular and what's not. You also found out how to view statistics and create custom searches for content.

Now, it's time to increase your feel for the asset marketplace. This time you'll look only at game assets.

Have a go hero – research the game asset marketplace

It's your turn to see what you can find out. There are a number of game asset marketplaces on the Internet. Look up a few of these and use their search functions to see what sells the most. You're most interested in high or medium-selling assets in these categories:

- High-selling, but easy to create.

- Assets that have no direct competition. If almost no one is selling this particular thing and there's a need for it, people will go for yours.

- High-selling assets that are poorly modeled. In other words, you can model a better one and get the sales!

- Areas that you're particularly interested in.

 Choose your niche
Don't just look for the highest selling models, but also for *what will sell the best for you.*

Just to get you going, try this:

1. Go to `http://www.google.com` and search for **3d game asset store** or similar. Start your research from there. You will no doubt encounter the **Unity Asset Store** which is accessed from within Unity. You can look at that one later on when you've installed **Unity 3D**. For now, try some others, like these:

   `http://www.turbosquid.com`

   `http://www.the3dstudio.com`

   `http://www.flatpyramid.com`

   `http://www.exchange3d.com`

2. Try to find the detailed search or equivalent on each of these sites (there always is one).

3. Type in the search area you're interested in, hit *enter*, and then order the search by popularity.

4. Add in the term "game ready" to your search to see if there's a category of assets devoted to games only.

5. Note down the differences between the game-ready and non-game ready assets.

Now, do the same sort of research you did in the 3D Warehouse, for each of the websites you find.

Your best CG textures source

Remember what the two most important things to consider are when creating game assets? It was in the quiz at the end of *chapter 1*. Good assets rely on good textures. The primary advice I can give here is to go and get a good compact camera and take texture photos wherever you go.

That is possibly the most important advice you can have as an asset creator. The reason you really need to do this yourself, rather than relying on a texture store, is that you can get textures and object photos at the same time. For the wooden pallet you'll be modeling in *Chapter 3, Wooden Pallet: Texture Creation*, you will need photos to create the textures, but also photos that show you how the object goes together. In fact, with SketchUp you can easily cheat and use the object photo as the texture photo too, using the great **PhotoMatch** tool you'll learn about in *Chapter 6, Importing to a Professional Game Application: Unity 3D*. Here, you'll learn how to directly create textures onto a model from a photo!

[The word **texture** is really defined as the surface quality of an object. In computer graphics, the term has come loosely to mean any image or graphic that is put onto a 3D surface. We'll be coming across textures a lot more in this book.]

Signing up to CGTextures.com

CGTextures.com is one of the best texture libraries available online. If you don't already have an account, go sign up for one today. First, it's completely free until you start using a serious amount of textures. Second, it's affordable when you need to upgrade to a full account. Finally, I'm going to use textures from the site in our tutorials, so you'll be able to download the same ones too.

Working this way in our tutorials ensures that you're developing all the skills that you need to create assets. That includes searching for and evaluating textured images. Nothing should be handed to you on a plate, because that's not how it works in the industry.

So, here we go!

1. Go to `http://www.cgtextures.com`.
2. Go to **Members ¦ Free Account**.
3. Fill in the form and click on **register**.
4. You'll need to wait for a confirmation e-mail.
5. Go to **Members ¦ Login** and use your new username and password to log in to the website.
6. You can now use the search box on the left-hand side to find what you want, or browse the library using the list of categories.

7. Click on a texture to view it. At the top of the window, you will see the following information:

Notice where it says **Quota left**. This shows you how many more images you can download using your free account during the current 24-hour period. This is gauged in Megabytes of data. When you select an image for download you can choose the size you need. Lower resolution images will use up less of your 15MB limit. However, be aware that when you get into game development for real you might find that lower resolutions can mean grainy looking textures once they're on your models.

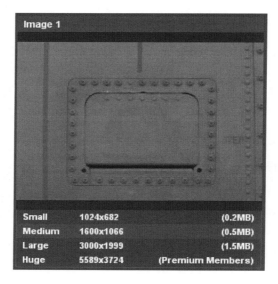

Copyright issues with textures

The other benefit of CGTextures.com is that they've got a copyright policy favorable to game asset developers. When choosing textures or photos from libraries make sure that they allow you to modify and distribute the textures with the assets. If your asset is used within a game, the copyright policy should allow the texture to be distributed within the game. You can check out their copyright policy by going to **About ¦ FAQ** and **About ¦ License**. The last thing you want is for your masterpiece Chinook helicopter to get pulled from Turbosquid because the texture isn't allowed to be distributed.

Here's a sample of what you should look out for:

CONDITIONS OF USE

Use of the Textures is only allowed under the following conditions:

- Private or commercial use

- Use in 2D or 3D computer graphics, movies and printed media

- Incorporation in computer games, 3D models

- Selling 3D models bundled with modified versions of the textures, when the texture is customized for the 3D model

It's the last two points that are most important to you, because you may be using the textures in your own games, but also selling the assets (along with textures) to be used as part of someone else's game.

Your library

Needless to say, you should be fastidious about where you save all your textures and images on your hard drive. Keep your own photos separate. These are your most flexible texture source because you own the copyright to them and don't need to worry about where they end up. Put photos from the other sources in different folders. Finally, within these folders classify images by subject or material. You might get a folder tree organized something like this one.

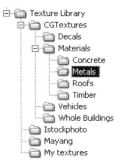

Meshlab

MeshLab can be useful. This tool is your 3D-geometry studio on a budget. With MeshLab, you can do some of the housekeeping tasks you need to do to take your SketchUp asset model and turn it into a game-ready article. It's completely free, but it's an "in development" project, so you might have to wrestle with it a little at times.

You can download Meshlab at `http://meshlab.sourceforge.net/`, and installation is straightforward. I recommend downloading the "stable" version. Go to the side menu and select the Windows, Mac, or Linux version from there.

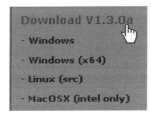

When you have installed the software, allow it to run, and you will get the following screen:

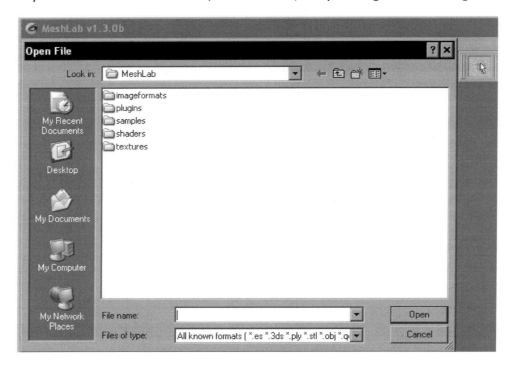

Time for action – learning about 3D meshes in MeshLab

Let's have a walk around MeshLab and learn some things about how assets are made up along the way. This will also help you to understand SketchUp better.

1. You don't have a SketchUp file to import yet, so go to the samples folder and open the `duck_triangulate.dae` file.

2. Your screen should look like the following. You'll learn what the individual buttons do as you progress through the book, and we'll only cover the stuff you really need.

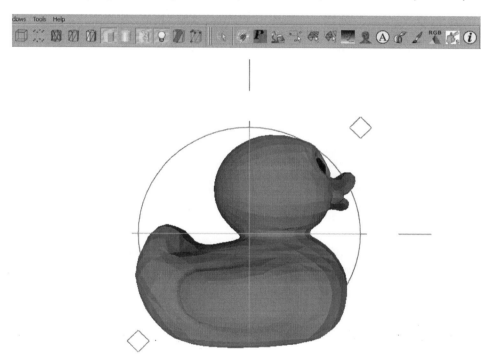

3. Here's the quintessential rubber ducky. You'll notice he looks as if he has been chiselled out roughly from stone. SketchUp modelers panic when they see this because they think everything needs to be smooth. What you are in fact seeing is polygons, and they're a good thing.

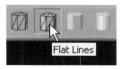

4.   Press the **Flat Lines** view style button now.

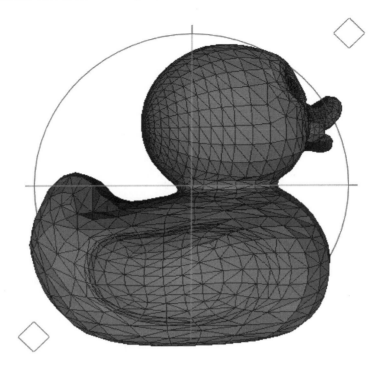

5.   You'll notice there's a line pattern on the duck. He now looks even worse than before! This view looks a little like a SketchUp model with **Hidden Geometry** switched on. SketchUp modelers also panic when they see lines in SketchUp because they think models should look smooth, textured, and fantastic right away. Some people stop trying 3D because they think there's something the professionals do that they can't do, and give up. They don't realize these lines and polygons are good.

6.   Why do you think MeshLab is called *MeshLab*? It's because all 3D models are made from a mesh. In fact, *any* shape in the world can be defined by a mesh. It's like taking some chicken mesh and pressing it over an object. If you then fill in all the gaps with plane surfaces, this is what you get. When you draw anything in SketchUp you are drawing a mesh, and when SketchUp detects a space with mesh round it, it automatically fills it in to create a surface. This surface is called a **polygon**.

7.   Now for the wow factor. Go to the next button (**Smooth**) and press it.

8. As you can see, the ducky isn't so messy after all.

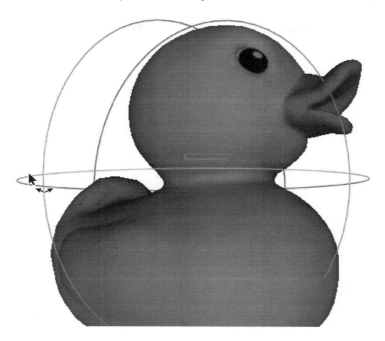

What just happened?

You installed MeshLab and took it for a brief test drive. You discovered that all 3D objects are made up of meshes. A mesh is made up of lines, making triangles. Whenever there is a triangle SketchUp and other 3D software create a surface, called a **Polygon**. The duck is made up of many polygons, and when we view it just like that all we see is a bunch of flat surfaces, which is of course what polygons are. MeshLab and other 3D software, such as rendering software, or gaming software, such as Unity 3D (see next section), will blend these polygons together to create a nice smooth surface.

Moving around in 3D

MeshLab can also teach you how to move around when modeling in 3D. Have you noticed the three rings round the duck? That's to help you see how to rotate in 3D. It represents a ball encompassing your model. Move your cursor over it now, left click, and hold the mouse button. Now, move left to right, up and down. As long as you remember this imaginary ball, you can visualize how to orbit your model in 3D space. It's as if the ball is fixed in the middle, and you're turning it by moving your hand over the surface like you would when spinning a globe.

File formats

The file format preferred by Unity 3D (see next section) is FBX. SketchUp Pro exports in this format, but doesn't import. Unfortunately MeshLab doesn't support it at all. Download the FBX Converter from **Autodesk** by going to http://usa.autodesk.com and enter **fbx converter** in the search box. Once you've installed this, you will be able to convert from 3DS, OBJ, DAE, and DXF to FBX format, and back again.

Get your game engine here: Unity 3D

Unity 3D has won the Wall Street Journal 2010 Technology Innovation Award in the software category, and Unity Technologies was named one of Gamasutra's "Top 5 Game Companies of 2009." Why? Because it's good.

What's Unity, and why's it free? Moreover, what do I need it for?

Download

Free Full Version for Windows with Unity Pro and Android trials.

Download Unity 3.4

System Requirements
License Comparison

Developing on Mac OS X?

Unity 3D is a Game development environment and **Game Engine**, technical term **Middleware**. Middleware is the software that game developers use to build their games on. It might surprise you to know that they rarely code a game from the ground up. They use Middleware, which is a combination of 3D rendering, Physics, sound, animation, artificial intelligence engines, and more. The game developers use this software and then pay the Middleware developers to allow them to ship their game with it. It runs in the background making all the bits and pieces work.

The reason you need Middleware is obvious, and the reason you need Unity 3D is that it provides arguably the best and most well-supported free one out there. There are some differences between the free and pay-for versions which you can check out at http://unity3d.com/unity/licenses.

The pro games environment

What this means really is that you're going to learn how to develop levels and assets for a true professional game environment. You will get an insight into how it all works if you were to work for a software house. Of course, these skills will naturally set you in good stead for all the less-demanding markets such as game-level modding. This is where you use simple tools bundled with commercial games to alter parts of the game or add to it.

Let's download it and see what a satisfying mess we can make in the pro gaming arena.

Time for action – obtaining Unity 3D for free

1. Go to `http://unity3d.com/unity/download/`.

2. Click on the **Download Unity Now** link and follow the instructions.

3. While you're downloading you will be presented with a page with more information on it. Click on the **Documentation** link.

Getting Started
If you're new to Unity, you should start here.

Basics
Learn the basic operation of Unity.

Community Forum
The ultimate resource for programmers, artists, game designers, and everyone else.

Tutorials
Printable, step-by-step guides covering various topics.

Video Tutorials
View these tutorials online or on your iPod.

Reference Material
Expand your knowledge... reach for the stars.

Example Projects
Downloadable projects for real-world examples. Feel free to use the assets in your own Unity games.

User Manual
The complete Unity manual. It is divided into sections for quick reference.

Reference Manual
Detailed information about every component in Unity.

Scripting Reference
Scripting overview and complete API reference with plentiful examples.

4. Come back to this page when you have time and browse all the learning material available.

5. When you've downloaded Unity, install and run it.

6. Click on **Register** when requested to do so.

7. Select **Internet Activation** (you will need to be connected to the Internet)

8. Enter your e-mail details.

9. Click on the **Free** license button.

10. Go back to your installation and click on **Finish**.

11. When you open Unity for the first time it should start importing the assets from the **Bootcamp** demo project.

12. When it's all done, go to **File ¦ Build & Run.**

13. Select **PC and Mac Standalone** (see next screenshot).

14. Select **Target Platform** (Windows or Mac).

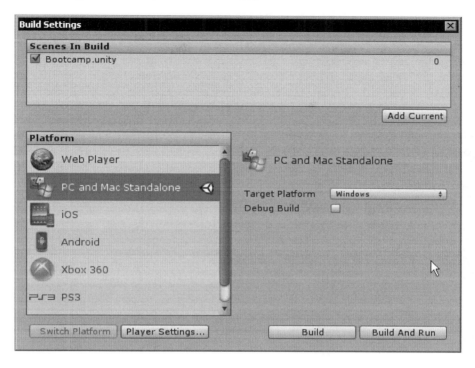

15. Click on **Build & Run** and enter a filename like `MyBootcamp`. Note the location where the file is being saved on your computer.

16. You're now going to test this example game level. Change your settings (shown below) to ensure it will work with your computer and graphics card.

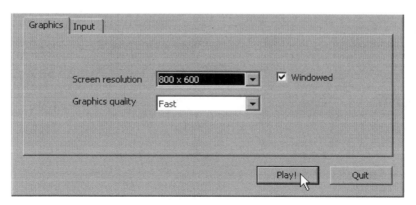

17. Click on **Play!**

18. Use the arrow keys to move and the mouse to look around.

19. When you're done playing around, hit escape and then click on the X at the top right-hand side of the window.

20. Now save the project by going to **File ¦ Save Project.**

What just happened?

You're now all set with an industry-respected game engine to test your assets and game levels. This software, combined with Google SketchUp, could ease you into a career in games design as a level designer or game asset artist.

 To see the difference between Unity and Unity Pro licenses, go to http://unity3d.com/unity/licenses.

Have a go hero – investigating the Unity sample assets

Now it's your turn to really begin focusing in on what assets are, what they're made from, and how they can be used effectively in game levels. Find the Bootcamp demo folder on your computer (you noted where it was when you typed in the MyBootcamp filename) and double-click on the game you compiled and played just now. You can keep returning to this to study how the Unity teams have put their level together, without having to compile and run from within Unity each time. From within the game, hit Escape. Go to Graphics and change Graphics Quality to **Fantastic**. Do you notice the difference compared to before?

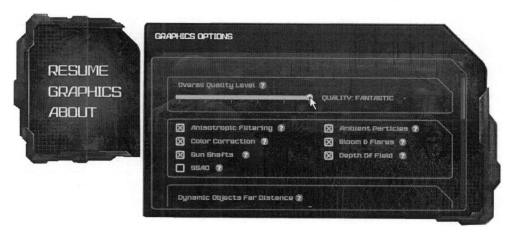

Use the arrow keys to walk over to each asset. Use your mouse to orbit around and get a close-up look all the way around each asset you find. Now answer these questions:

- How would I go about modeling this asset?
- Is it made up of **flat** or **solid** geometry?
- If solid, how many faces (polygons) does it have?
- If flat, is it crisp or fuzzy up close?
- Does the whole asset have separate component parts?
- How detailed is it really when you look up close?

- Is the effect better when you see it from a distance?

As with any discipline, the more thoroughly you investigate what's already been done before, the better you will be at creating your own.

Google SketchUp

This one needs no introduction, and I'm going to assume you've already got SketchUp installed on your system because installation is straightforward. Instead, I'll use the space allocated to SketchUp installation telling you about the extra texture pack you can have that will enhance SketchUp even more.

Here's how to find and install the extra textures provided by Google.

Enhanced texture packs

Once you have SketchUp or SketchUp Pro installed, go to `http://sketchup.google.com/intl/en/download/bonuspacks6.html` and click on the download link for Windows or Mac. Run the file and follow the instructions.

Component Library	# of items	file size	Windows	Mac OS X
Architecture	723	12.7 MB	Download	Download
Construction	797	6 MB	Download	Download
Film & Stage	107	3.4 MB	Download	Download
Landscape Architecture	583	14.3 MB	Download	Download
People	166	5.7 MB	Download	Download
Symbols	26	1.9 MB	Download	Download
Transportation	48	3 MB	Download	Download

Materials Library	# of items	file size	Windows	Mac OS X
Materials Bonus Pack	626	14.4 MB	Download	Download

When you're asked where to install the texture pack, click on the **Change** button and select your **Google SketchUp 8** folder.

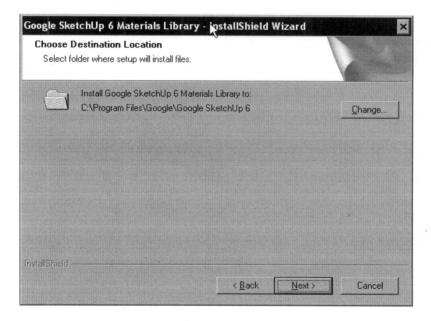

Six hundred additional textures will automatically install for you to use in your game assets and levels! You can access them in the Materials pallet as you can see here.

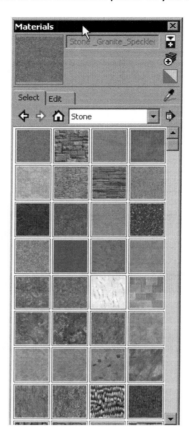

GIMP: The free professional graphics editor

Much of the asset creation process involves manipulation of images, textures and photos, so you need a professional-level image editor. GIMP is an **open source** graphics editor which in the past was based mostly on Adobe Photoshop. That means if you've done graphics work before in Photoshop, you should be able to recognize most of the functions in GIMP. The reason we're using GIMP in this book is that not everyone has access to Photoshop, which is a costly piece of software, and lower cost versions such as Photoshop Elements just don't have the functions required to do asset creation. If you have Photoshop installed, you can use that instead without too much difficulty, as Photoshop has all the functions of GIMP and more.

To install GIMP go to `http://www.gimp.org` and click on the **download** link. The Windows installer should be at the top of the list. For the MAC version click on **show other downloads** and scroll down to **GIMP for Mac OS X**.

Now it's time to check you've not been napping through this whole chapter, with a quick quiz.

Pop quiz – tools you'll need for asset creation

1. Name three asset marketplaces on the Internet.

2. What assets tend to sell best on these internet marketplaces?

3. Do game assets look detailed when you view them close up, or are they better when viewed from a distance?

4. What's the name given to the geometry that makes up a 3D asset?

5. True or false: I need to design assets with a lot of polygons in order to get smooth surfaces?

6. True or false: Tools that are free on the internet aren't of sufficient quality to use in your asset creation workflow?

If you need any help on these questions, quickly review the chapter before moving on. This chapter forms the basis of the tutorials in the rest of the book. Each chapter that follows builds on the previous ones until you have achieved a functioning game level complete with all its contents.

Summary

We're just about done with chapter, as well as downloading great software, what else have we learned?

- How to research existing assets to find out what sells well.

- Beginning your personal textures database

- What meshes, polygons, faces, and smoothing mean to you.

- Installing a professional game development environment

- How 2D and 3D assets are constructed.

In the next chapter, you will get started making your first asset in SketchUp—a textured wooden pallet. You will learn lots of SketchUp's functions along the way. You will then import it to Unity to see how it looks in a game environment!

3
Wooden Pallet: Texture Creation

In this first tutorial, you will create a texture that is ready for modeling as we move into the next chapter. We'll use these two chapters together as a complete tutorial on the asset creation process from beginning to end.

In this first tutorial, you will learn how to:

- Turn a photo into a photo texture material
- Straighten and manipulate photos
- Run filters to enhance color, contrast, and sharpness
- Combine multiple textures into one master texture
- Prepare your texture for gaming

Finding textures to use in asset modeling

It's time to select a texture and prepare it for modeling into a 3D object. You're going to find your texture on CGTextures.com and model straight from that, giving you the best realism possible. Also, this means you don't need to worry about finding measurements of things; you can model by eye.

Time for action – selecting the photo texture

1. Set up a project folder somewhere on your computer called `Pallet`. Within that folder create a folder called `Textures` and one called `Meshes`.

2. Go to `http://www.cgtextures.com` and sign in with the username and password you set up in *Chapter 2*, *Tools that Grow on Trees*, by going to **Members ¦ Login**.

3. Above the list of categories to the left-hand side, there's a search box. Enter **pallet** and search.

4. Select a good top-down view of a pallet that's not too clean. The next screenshot shows the pallet we're going for in this tutorial.

5. When you click on the thumbnail image it should list the texture as **Cargo0070**. Select **Large.**

6. In the popup box, select **Save File** and save the image in your `Pallet` project folder.

7. Now close this window and navigate to the list of categories on the left-hand side. Click **Wood ¦ Ends**.

8. Select one of the thumbnails. Hover the cursor over the image to get a larger view.

9. Hold down *z* to see a zoomed in area. As you can see with this one, the details are too blurry.

Selecting images

When selecting photo textures, look for ambient lighting without hard shadows, plenty of interesting detail, and crisp, in-focus images.

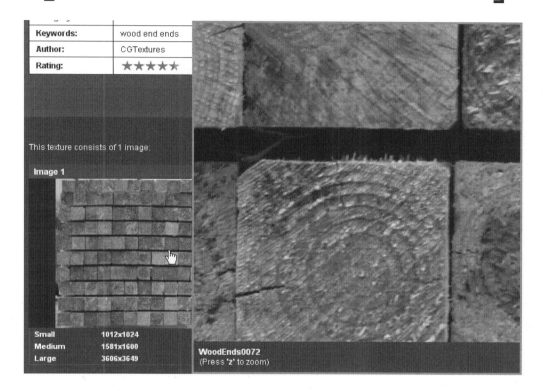

Keywords:	wood end ends
Author:	CGTextures
Rating:	★★★★★

This texture consists of 1 image:

Image 1

Small	1012x1024
Medium	1581x1600
Large	3606x3649

WoodEnds0072
(Press 'z' to zoom)

10. Look through the thumbnails until you find a crisp, clear image that you think will work well for the wood ends on the pallet. I'm going for **WoodEnds0060**. Save your chosen image in your `Pallet` project folder.

What just happened

You now have two high-resolution textures in your `Pallet` folder. These are base textures that you will use to create the textures that will adorn your model. Base textures are never used as they are without modification. You first need to ready them for game use. This will include:

1. Enhancing tone, brightness, and white balance
2. Running filters to sharpen the focus
3. Cropping, straightening, and resizing
4. Compressing and saving in the correct file format

This might seem like a lot to do just for a game texture, but bear in mind the usefulness of an asset is 90% down to the texturing. If you get this part right, you're setting yourself up for success. Besides it's actually really quick and easy, as you'll now see.

Enhancing textures

You're now going to make game-ready textures using GIMP.

1. Open GIMP and go to **File ¦ Open.**
2. Select the **Cargo0070** image and open it.

Take a look at the image and think about the four processes that you just read about. Which ones do you think need to be done, and in what order? Let's go through the whole thing and then see at the end why we did it this way.

Time for action – cropping and enhancing

1. The pallet looks quite square already. Click on the ruler at the left-hand side of the image, hold down the left mouse button as you do so, and move the mouse to the right.

2. This sets up a vertical ruler guide. You can move this until it's at the left-hand side edge of the pallet. As you can see, it's completely horizontal.

3. Do the same with the right-hand side edge, and then use the horizontal ruler at the top of the image to set up the horizontal guides at the top and bottom edges. See the result in the next image.

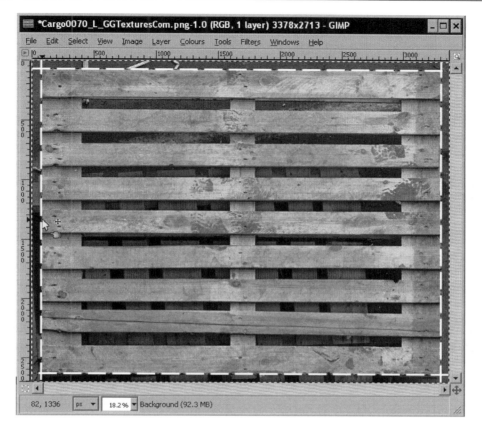

4. As you can see, the texture does not need any more straightening. You have now set up four rulers which you can work with. Click on the **Crop** Tool in the main tool pallet.

5. Click on the bottom left-hand side corner where the guides cross, and then drag to the top right-hand side. Hit *Enter* to crop the image.

6. Now to enhance the colors. Go to **Colours ¦ Auto ¦ White Balance**.

 You can try any of the options in the **Auto** menu to enhance the contrast or color quality in your image. Some will work better than others depending on the image you're editing.

7. Go to **Image ¦ Scale Image**.

8. Type **1024** into the **Width** box. The **Height** field updates automatically.

9. Select **Sinc (Lanczos3)** in the box marked **Interpolation**.

10. Click on the **Scale** button.

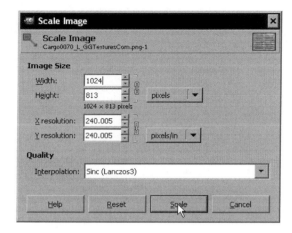

11. To change the zoom, change the value in the small box located at the bottom of the main window. Try setting it to **100%**. You have now zoomed in to the highest level of detail contained in this image.

12. Go to **Filters ¦ Enhance ¦ Unsharp Mask**. Click on **OK** to use the default settings.

13. Go to **File ¦ Undo** and **File ¦ Redo** to look at the difference before and after using this filter.

14. Go to **Image ¦ Canvas Size**.

15. Click the chain icon at the side of the **Width** and **Height** fields. Type in **1024** in the **Height** field.

16. Click on **Centre**. Notice the preview image of the pallet moves to the center of the canvas? Now type in **0** into the **Y** field to move the pallet to the top of the canvas.

17. Click on **Resize**.

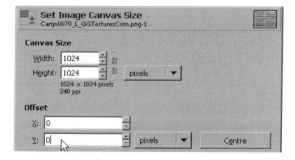

18. You have now finished the process for the top of the pallet. Go to **File ⁞ Save As** and find the words **Select File Type**. Click on the plus sign next to it.

19. You now have a list of file formats to choose from. Select **GIMP XCF Image**. It will retain all your image data.

20. Click on **Save**.

 When saving an image-based project, never save to the original file format, so use **Save As**, and not **Save**. Use the **GIMP XCF** format, which retains all parts of your image project, such as layers, masks, and paths. We will come across these later in this book. Other formats such as PNG and JPG do not retain these elements..

What just happened?

You've created your first game texture, and a good one at that!

- You made sure the object was square and straight by using ruler guides.

- You used the guides as references while using the **Crop Tool** to change the image size.

- You resized to 1024 pixels wide. This is small enough to keep the file size down, while being one of the recommended standard file sizes.

- You enhanced the image contrast by using the **Auto White Balance** filter.

- You enhanced image sharpness by using **Unsharp Mask.**

- You resized the image canvas to make it a square of 1024 x 1024 pixels and made sure the image was positioned at the top of the canvas.

All this won't take you two minutes per texture once you get into it. You've now learned the most useful basic image manipulation skills, and you've had a walk around GIMP to see that it's really not as unfriendly as it might look.

 You can access the texture you've got so far in the Download Pack, labeled `Chapter3stage01.xcf`

What are pixels?

All digital images are made up of thousands of dots of color, arranged in a grid. A pixel is the smallest part of that grid. So, a 1024-pixel wide image has 1024 dots in each row of dots. If the image is also 1024 pixels high, it has 1024 of these rows, making a little over 1 million dots, or pixels.

What you are doing by manipulating an image is changing the color or shade in many individual dots at the same time. If you type in **2000** into the zoom field and hit *Enter*, you can see these individual pixels in your texture image. If you hold the book at arms length and squint a little you'll see the colored pixels make up a nail in the wood.

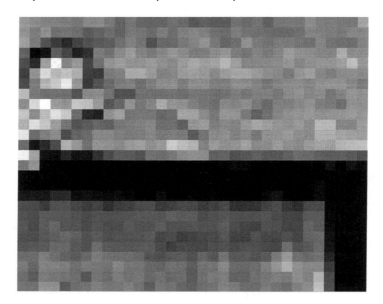

Texture sizes

The reason you resized to 1024 x 1024 pixels is because the image you had was too large (it held too much information) and so had a large file size. In gaming, we have to be constantly aware of the speed at which the game will render while playing it, so graphics file size is a big issue. In fact, 1024 isn't the final size you'll end up with. Later, you might decide to resize to 256 or 128 pixels wide. After all, a timber pallet is unlikely to be the showcase feature in your game level!

Textures should also be square if possible or a ratio of 2:1 or 1:2, such as 512 x 1024. For computer game graphics reasons, it is standard to make all graphics a **power-of-two** size. Get the number 2 and keep doubling it, and any of the sizes you get are ok (64, 128, 256, 512, 1024, 2048, 4096, and so on). This is traditionally because the computer memory allocates memory to textures in blocks of a power of two, so having a 520x520 image would still take up 1024x1024 of memory. Two of the more tangible benefits of this are that you work to standard sizes, cutting down the amount of decisions you have to make, and you can easily resize your texture to a range of file sizes by simply halving it a few times in GIMP.

Time for action – arranging multiple textures

You may have noticed that you have a clear space at the bottom of your texture. This is where you're now going to arrange some more textures, namely the wood ends of the pallet. The reasons for putting them on the same texture are:

- Ease of use when modeling

- Economical on file size (using all of the memory block allocated to the texture)

- Better in game graphics performance

- You don't need to work on multiple files when resizing or changing color or shade

- Easier to bundle with the asset

I'm sure there are many more you can think of too. If nothing else, this keeps everything neat and tidy. If you end up with a game level with 500 assets in it, do you prefer 500 textures to go with it, or 5000? Things can get messy very quickly. So, on behalf of your future employer, I counsel you to texture in this way! Here's an example from the Bootcamp Demo level-bundled with Unity 3D. It's a 1024x1024 size image, and as you can see, every available space is used so that every bit of the allocated texture memory block is used too.

1. Find the second texture you downloaded and saved from: `http://www.cgtextures.com` earlier.

2. Open it in GIMP as before.

3. Zoom in to 100% and use the sidebars to scroll around the image. Can you find a sharply focused, interesting timber end?

4. Use the **Crop** tool to crop round a timber end, as shown next, leaving some space around the edge. Hit *Enter* to complete the action.

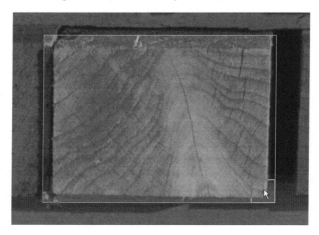

5. Set up your four guides as you did before, dragging them from the side rulers with your mouse.

6. You'll notice that this time the edges are not perfectly vertical and horizontal, as you can see in this screenshot:

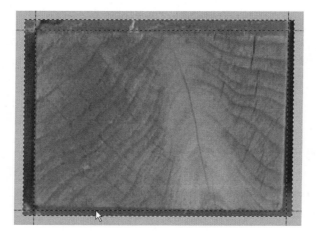

7. You need to stretch the wood end so that all the sides and corners line up with the horizontal and vertical guides. To do this, select the **Perspective** Tool.

8. Click near a corner and hold the mouse button down. Drag to change the shape of the image. You can see this being done at the bottom right-hand side of the next screenshot.

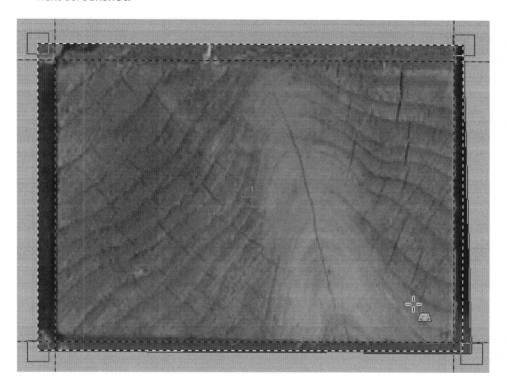

9. This way, it's a simple task to go around each corner and stretch the wood end to fit squarely into the guides you've created.

10. You can take as long as you like over this, because the actual image doesn't changed until you click on: `http://www.cgtextures.com`.

11. When you have finished, click on the **Transform** button in the **Perspective** part of the **Toolbox** window, and then use the **Crop** Tool like before to crop the image to the guides.

12. Go to **Image ¦ Scale Image** and resize using **Width** of **256** pixels.

13. Go to **Filters ¦ Enhance ¦ Unsharp Mask** to sharpen the grain. You already know how to do this from the previous example.

14. Go to **Select ¦ All** and then **Edit ¦ Copy**.

15. Switch to your original pallet texture project, or open it in GIMP.

16. Go to **Edit ¦ Paste**. The wood end texture will appear over the top of the pallet texture.

17. Make sure the **Layers**, **Channels**, **Paths**, **Undo** pallet is visible. If not, you can open it using the **Windows** menu. You can see what it looks like below.

18. Right-click your mouse on the part that says **Floating Selection** and select **New Layer** (or alternatively select **Layer ¦ New Layer** from the main **Layer** menu). This fixes your new texture to a new layer, distinct from the pallet texture.

19. Using the **Move** Tool, click and drag the mouse to place the new texture under the pallet texture.

Layers

Now that you have a new *layer* with the wood end texture on it, anything you do in GIMP will only affect that Layer. Layers can be thought of sheets of clear plastic, one on top of another. You can control which Layer you're working on by selecting the Layer you want in the **Layers Pallet**.

20. Notice that the color of the wood is different from the pallet texture. This will make your model look wrong. You can remedy this by either going to **Colour ¦ Auto ¦ White Balance** or for a more controlled effect, go to **Colour ¦ Hue-Saturation** and alter the **Saturation** value.

21. You should have something like this for your finished texture:

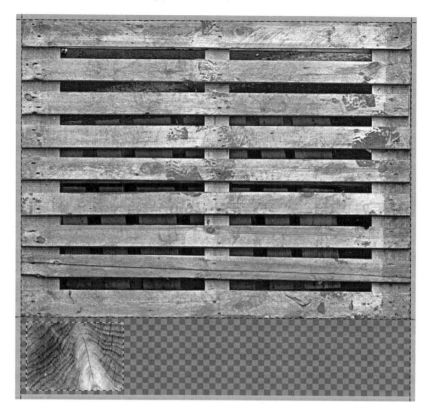

Have a go hero

Now it's your turn to repeat these steps a few times and complete the texture set. Go back to your wood ends project and click on the **Undo** tab of the **Layers, Channels, Paths, and Undo** pallets. Here, you have a list of actions you performed with the image. Go to the top of the list and select the item named **Base Image** which will return the project back to the original image. You can now repeat the steps above a few other times to create two more wood ends, and paste them into the main project.

Saving textures

When you are done, save the finished project as a **GIMP XCF** image as before. This retains all the different layers so that you can work on them some time later if you need to. You are now also going to create a few versions of the texture to use on your SketchUp model. These can be in TGA, TIF, or BMP format.

Naming conventions

When you buy an asset, you want to know that you can use the asset straight out of the box. You also need to know you can modify it easily in the future, should you need to. An asset is exactly what the name implies—an asset to you or your company. It holds value and is stored for later use again and again. In order to make things easy for whomever ends up using your asset, you should name the textures and meshes something easily recognizable. Texture names should follow the format:

```
asset_feature_size.format
```

So for a car asset, you might name the headlamp texture, sized at 256x256 pixels as

```
astonmartin_headlight_256.tga
```

For your Pallet asset, you will be creating two versions of your texture; a low- and high-resolution version. You should name them `pallet_wood_256.tga` and `pallet_wood_1024.tga`, respectively.

Copyright text

In order to avoid your texture appearing all over the Internet as a free download, it is useful to add a **by-line** to the file. This small line of text shows who created the texture, where you can go to get some more like it, and also gives credit where it's due. For example, the website CGTextures.com asks us to name them as the source of the texture, as does anyone providing images under the **Creative Commons attribution license**. You might get images like this from Flickr.com

Time for action – final touches

1. You're almost there! In your GIMP project, click on the **New Layer** icon at the bottom of the Layers pallet.

2. When prompted, select **Foreground Color** under **Layer Fill Type**.

3. Click on **OK**.

4. In the **Layers** pallet, click and drag the black layer you created so that it sits at the bottom of the list.

5. Click on the **Text Tool** and click in some spare space at the bottom right of your image. Type in your text. Change text size as required using the **Size** field, as you can see in the following screenshot.

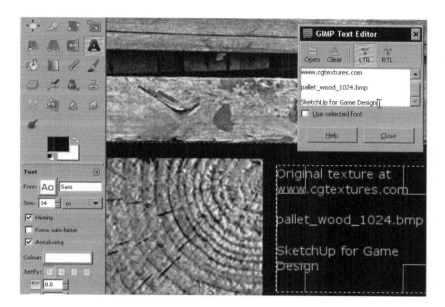

6. Click the **Colour** field and select the white color.

7. Stretch the text box to fit the space you have available, as visible in the screenshot.

8. Your texture project is now finished. Click on **File ¦ Save.**

9. Now it's time to save several sizes to use in your SketchUp model. Go to **Image ¦ Flatten Image.**

10. Select **File ¦ Save As**. Navigate to the folder you named **Textures**.

11. In the **Name** field, type in **pallet_wood_1024.tga** and click on **Save**.

12. Select **Origin ¦ Bottom Left.**

13. Now resize your texture to 512x512 pixels as you did before. Save this as `pallet_ wood_512.tga`.

What just happened?

You've saved your master project as a GIMP XCF file which you will be able to alter again later if you wish. You've flattened the image to get rid of the individual layers, and saved the file twice as a simple flat image in Targa (`.tga`) format. These are the textures you will use, they and won't be altered again.

 You can find the finished GIMP project and final texture in the download pack labelled `Chapter3_pallet_texture.xcf` and `PalletWood_1024.tga`.

Summary

In this chapter, you have learned all about texture creation starting from a base photo, and how to work on it in GIMP to produce a game-ready master texture. Along the way, you learned about image formats, pixels, useful GIMP functions, filters, and lots more. We'll continue the tutorial in *Chapter 4, Wooden Pallet: Modeling*, where you'll learn to model the asset from your texture.

4

Wooden Pallet: Modeling

Didn't you just love the summer holidays as a kid? Didn't they just stretch out in front of you like an eternity full of promise? Not so much for your mom or dad, though. Well, I think my mom must have gotten fed up of me after one week because she checked me into a summer activity school. I wasn't happy, I can tell you... until I got there. The supervisor opened a door into the largest junkyard I had ever seen, only this one didn't have cars, but wood. Everywhere you looked kids had been let loose and were building dens, climbing frames, towers, go-carts , you name it. The supervisor gestured towards a set of woodworking benches and beside them there were racks and racks of hammers, saws, chisels, planes, files, and many more items. "Help yourself," he said, "and you'll need plenty of these," as he shoved a huge tin of nails into my small hands. I think I was only six, but I didn't notice my mom leave.

Making assets for games is a bit like a young boy's dream activity holiday. You have all the wood you want, all the shiny new tools you need of every make, model and size, and a huge supply of nails. When you need more, the supervisor just fills your tin up. All we know about the monetary cost is that someone's paid for it all. The only limits are our time and ingenuity.

When you get the hang of modeling with SketchUp, you will be able to model more or less whatever you or your boss want. Time's the only limit. We can fill the world if we want to, and that's actually what it's all about. Your game needs to be like the real world, full of stuff, mostly junk. The asset stores unfortunately have mostly good stuff, when what you really want is bits of wood with nails sticking out, old tanks of decaying vegetables, buildings with plaster and tiles falling off. These things make your worlds real. You get these assets simply by taking pictures of the junk in your world, then transferring it to your game world through SketchUp. You might modify them a little too, to accentuate certain things. In this first modeling tutorial, you will learn how to:

- Model from your texture, not texture your model
- Extrude 2D shapes into 3D shapes with **Push/Pull**
- Use **Copy** and **Move**, and some hidden features of these tools
- Create groups and components to create quick duplicates
- Use most of the basic modeling tools in SketchUp

...and much more! You should pick up skills and techniques as you go along without really noticing. So let's get started!

Your first model in SketchUp

You've already installed SketchUp and I hope you're dying to get started with modeling. The texturing part took a while to explain, but now you know what you're doing with textures, you'll always be well prepared for modeling tasks. The approach to modeling in this book is to use photo or image textures as a base, rather than modeling first and texturing later. It is a much easier approach than the traditional one, and well-suited to SketchUp. When you begin creating more advanced models and textures in *Chapter 7, Quick Standard Assets* , and *Chapter 9, The Main Building—Inside and Out*, you will also learn how to adapt photo textures in GIMP using the original photos as a base. Of course, if you're an artistic soul you can go on from there and create textures from scratch, but I suggest you first need to know how to do it this way before you venture out into that new world.

SketchUp get-up-and-get-started guide

When you open SketchUp for the first time, you need to select a template and get yourself used to moving around in 3D. I've covered some of these more basic start-up topics at http://www.sketchupuser.com/basics.

Time for action – importing a texture to scale

1. Open up SketchUp and go to **Window ¦ Preferences**, then select the **Template** option.

2. Select **Engineering – Meters** and click on **Start using SketchUp**.

3. You can now see the main SketchUp window. You can use the person displayed in the main window to help you visualize scale. Leave her there for the moment.

4. For this first tutorial, you will also need the **Views** and **View Styles** menu bars, so go to **View ¦ Toolbars** and make sure **Views** and **Styles** are checked in the list.

5. You can drag these toolbars where you wish. When you drag them onto the side or top of the SketchUp window, they will **dock** and stay there.

6. Alternatively you can access them via menus by selecting **View ¦ Face Style** and **Camera ¦ Standard Views**.

7. Go to **File ¦ Import** and select your texture, `pallet_wood_1024.tga`. Check **Use as Image** and click on **Open**.

8. Move the cursor until it snaps to the origin. It will display the text **Origin** as you can see next.

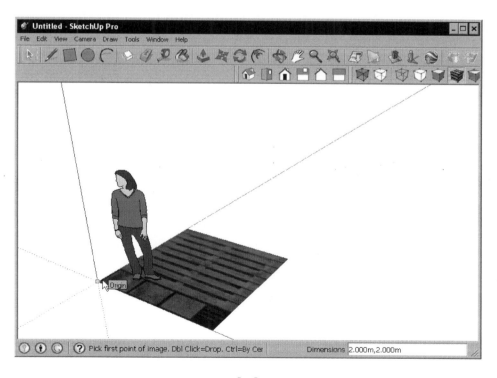

9. Click here and move the mouse to resize the image. Click again when the image looks about the right size for a pallet in relation to the person.

10. Click the person and hit **delete**.

11. Now we need to resize the pallet more exactly. Click on the **Tape Measure Tool** button. Click on one corner of the texture and then move along the longest side of the pallet and click again at the corner.

12. This gives you the current measurement of the texture. Now type in the measurement you want this to be. Type `1.2` and hit *Enter*.

13. When asked to resize the model, click on **Yes**.

14. Go to **Camera ¦ Parallel Projection**. Now click the **Top** view button. You can now see the texture from top down.

15. Go to **File ¦ Save** and type in the filename `pallet_MASTER`. Click on **Save**.

What just happened?

You have set up a SketchUp project with the filename `pallet_MASTER` in which you will do all your modeling. You will create the finished asset later, or several versions of it, from this main file, but the file itself remains only accessible to you. You set the units to meters and imported your texture image to start modeling from.

Modeling from the texture

Your texture is correctly scaled because it was taken from a photo of a real world object. So, when you provide the measurement of only one side of it, the rest is also okay. All you need to do now is transfer this two-dimensional texture into a three-dimensional SketchUp model, or **Mesh**. You do this by drawing shapes over the texture and then pulling them into a 3D shape.

Time for action – basic 3D geometry

1. Right click on the texture image and select **Explode**. This turns the image into a rectangle of geometry that you can model with.

2. Use the mouse wheel to zoom in to the bottom left-hand side of the pallet. Click on the **Line** tool, or press *L*.

3. Move the tool over the edge of the photo and notice that the pencil snaps to the edge, and shows an **On Edge** prompt (as you can see here).

4. With the pencil still snapped to the edge, find the corner of the pallet and click.

5. Find the other corner of the pallet to the right and click again. You can zoom out with the wheel, and pan by holding *Shift* and pressing the middle mouse button (usually the same as the mouse wheel).

6. Notice that the horizontal line turns red to show you it's snapping to the horizontal.

7. Zoom out, and then select the **Eraser** button or press *E*. Click on the shaded view button. You can see that the bottom rectangle is made up of lines and two light blue or grey faces.

8. Erase the left, right, and bottom lines that enclose the bottom face. Notice that the face disappears, too.

9. You should now have only the top rectangle with the pallet in it. Click on the **Shaded with Textures** view button to see the texture again. Press the spacebar to turn off the **Eraser**.

10. Double-click on the rectangle. Right click and select **Make Component**. Type in
`pallet_boards`. Make sure **Replace selection with component** is selected and
click on **Create**.

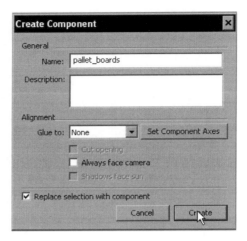

11. Click on the **Move** button. Select the bottom left-hand side corner and move it to
the origin. Click on again.

12. Double-click on the Component to edit it. Press *L* for Line.

13. Zoom in to the left edge and draw a line from the left edge to the right edge that
follows the first plank of wood.

14. Repeat this for all planks of wood.

15. If your line turns red to snap to the horizontal, but you want a slightly off-horizontal line, zoom in further to the edge and you will be able to make finer adjustments to the line.

16. When you've finished, use the eraser to delete all the rectangles between the wood planks. Delete first the left lines, then the right (see the next screenshot).

What just happened?

You've made a component which consists of the top planks for the pallet. You traced the geometry from the image with the line tool that has created one face for each plank. A component is an intelligent group of SketchUp geometry, and you will see what it does in a minute. Do remember to save your model.

Hold the middle mouse button and move the mouse up and to the left. The model orbits around. Orbiting in 3D is what you learned when you installed MeshLab in *Chapter 2, Tools that Grow on Trees*. Remember to think about an invisible globe wrapped around your model. When you move the mouse, you spin the globe with your hand. You will notice that the pallet is still only flat, even though you can view the flat geometry in 3D. You're now going to give it some thickness.

The orbit tool

If you don't have a middle mouse button, you can access the orbit tool by going to **Camera ¦ Orbit**, clicking on the **Orbit** button, or simply typing '*O*' (for Orbit) on the keyboard.

Time for action – Push/Pull, Move, and Copy

The **Push/Pull** tool in SketchUp is where most of the fun really begins. It's just great to see 2D stuff becoming 3D! It's as easy as this:

1. Double-click in the **Component** to begin modifying it. Now select the **Push / Pull** tool.

2. Hover over the top of a plank until it highlights blue, and click. Now when you move the mouse, you can extrude the flat geometry into a 3D box.

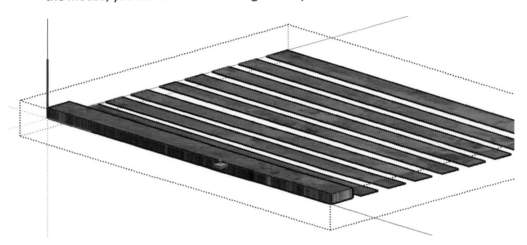

3. Make sure the extrusion is going upwards, as you can see in the previous screenshot. Now click. You could leave it like this, but to Push/Pull to a particular dimension, type in 0.02 and hit *Enter*. You must do this during or directly after you use **Push/Pull** for it to work.

4. Did you notice the plank jumped to the size you specified? Now double-click on each plank to repeat this command. SketchUp remembers the dimension you last used!

5. You now have a set of 3D planks saved as a component.

Components

A component can be copied as many times as you like, and any changes you later make to it will affect all copies. So, in this case, you will copy the planks to form the bottom of the pallet, even though you know there's some more texturing to be done. You will also find components and groups useful for separating geometry into discrete groups so that it doesn't all stick together.

6. Hit the *spacebar* and then double-click somewhere outside the component. This is how you stop editing a component or group.

7. Select the **Move** tool. This also works for copying stuff. All you have to do is press *Ctrl* (*Option* on Mac) some time during the move operation, and it will **copy** instead. Give this a go now.

8. Click on the planks component and press *Ctrl* (*Option* on Mac). There are now two copies. Move the mouse down until you see a blue-dotted line and click.

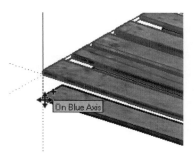

9. The **tooltip** will show **On Blue Axis**, reminding you that if you click now you can be assured the copy went only in the Up/Down direction.

Inference

Inference is a key innovation of SketchUp over other CAD software, and many other programmers have now adopted this approach because it works so well. Rather than having to enter exact coordinates all the time in 3D space, SketchUp developers realized most of the time we just wanted to move stuff either up, down, left, right, in or out. The colored axes in SketchUp will appear any time you're manipulating or creating anything to guide you along any one of these 6 directions.

10. Now type in 0.15 and the copy will jump that distance on the blue axis.

11. Orbit the model so that you're looking almost end-on, like the next screenshot.

12. Now select the **Rectangle** tool and click on the bottom left corner of the uppermost plank. Click somewhere on the top of the lower plank as shown here.

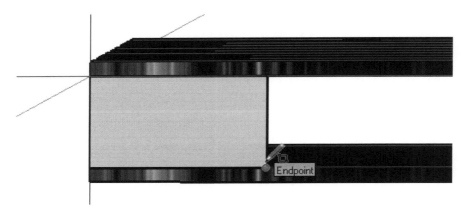

13. Select the **Push/Pull** tool and click on the rectangle. Extrude it and click anywhere on the back of the pallet. The tooltip will say **On Edge in Component**.

What just happened?

You've just completed creating the 3D geometry of your pallet without even breaking into a sweat! That's because modeling is so easy with SketchUp. You're going to be good at this, trust me.

You've just learned how to use **Push/Pull**, **Move**, **Copy**, **Inference**, the **Line** tool, the **Rectangle** tool, creating **Components**, and so on. In fact, all the main SketchUp modeling tools!

It's really that easy!

You can now really see your pallet taking shape. You're only partway through the first modeling chapter and already you have learned how to use all the most common modeling tools in SketchUp. It has been well within your own capabilities, am I right? In fact, this is all the modeling you need to do to make this 3D game asset.

When you go on from here, you will realize all the complex models you see in hi-tech 3D games have been made by breaking the modeling into simple smaller tasks like the one you've just completed. All geometry is, after all, just boxes and curves. You'll learn everything you need to know about simple and complex curves in *Chapter 5, Game Levels in SketchUp* and *Chapter 8, Advanced Modeling: Create a Realistic Car in Easy Steps*, but you should realize most geometry you need to create for assets and levels doesn't need that complex stuff.

Time for action – multiple copies

The neat thing about SketchUp is that you can do a lot more with it than is immediately apparent. The reason it's been designed this way is that it keeps a pleasant and uncluttered visual interface. Let's look at one such hidden feature now that will make a big difference in your modeling from now on.

1. Press the spacebar to go back to the default **Select** tool. Triple click on one of the faces of the timber member you just made. This will select all the geometry connected to that face.

2. Select the **Move** tool and click at the bottom right of the timber member, as shown next.

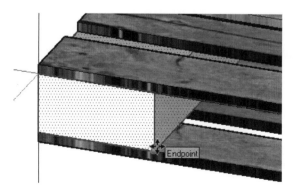

3. Now press *Ctrl* (*Option* on the Mac) and move the copy to the bottom right-hand corner of the pallet, and click again. You now have two members, one at each side of the pallet.

4. So far so good! But what about one in the middle? Use the move tool and hover the cursor near the bottom center of the extrusion. The cursor snaps to the midpoint of the line (see next).

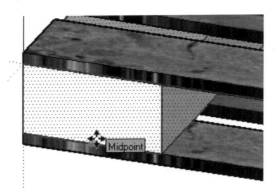

5. Click here, tap *Ctrl (Option on the Mac)*, and move towards the center of the pallet. When you see the dotted line going red and the tooltip **On Edge in Component**, hold down the *Shift* key. This restricts your movement to that edge only.

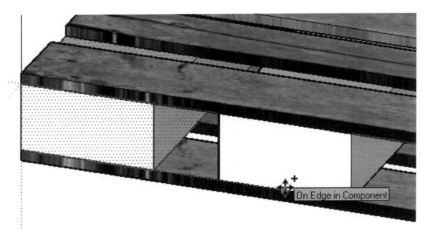

6. Notice wherever you move your mouse, the object stays locked to that edge. Now move to roughly the middle of the pallet, and click when the Tooltip says **Midpoint in Component**.

7. This is one way of doing it. There's another that's even better. First, triple click and delete the middle and right-hand side members you just created.

8. Triple click the left-hand side member and copy it to the right-hand side end as you did before. Now, before you do anything else, type in **/2** and press *Enter*. A copy appears in the middle. Now type **/4** and press *Enter*.

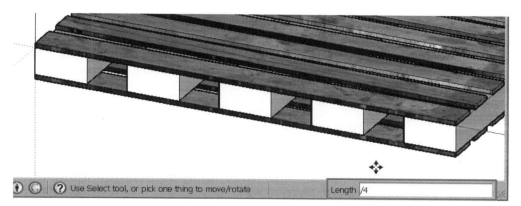

9. Anything you type with a forward slash in front of it will divide the space you moved into that many spaces. So, you now have four spaces, and five members equally spaced.

10. You can see the number you typed in the box at bottom right of the window. Type **/2** now to revert back to the two spaces you require.

What just happened?

You found a hidden feature, or tool subset, of SketchUp that allowed you to copy objects multiple times with equal spacing between them. This is really useful when you have a space to fill but don't know how many objects you need to fill it with. You also learned some more about Inference, by snapping to endpoint, midpoint and edges, and how to lock inferencing by pressing the *Shift* key.

The power of pre-prepared textures

When you think about it, your pallet is only a few simple rectangles that you Push/Pulled into box shapes. The realism is provided by the texture you created. This is how it should be. Complex geometry doesn't sit well with gaming because of the strain it puts on the gaming engine and your computer processor. Textures are a "low overhead" way of adding realism.

You're now going to experience just how powerful this method is, by adding subtle shadows and shading with a *single click* of your mouse.

Time for action – completing texturing

1. In SketchUp go to **Window** and click **Materials**. The **Materials Pallet** appears.

2. Click on the *Home* icon (see next image). Here you have a list of all materials being used in your current model.

 The Mac version has an additional selection of color pallets at the top of the window. Select the symbol for **SketchUpColorPicker** to get the same pallet as the Windows one shown here.

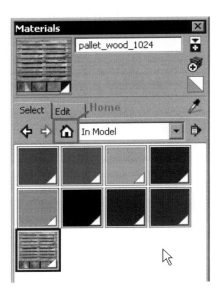

3. Notice that your `pallet_wood_1024` texture has automatically become a material, and you didn't even need to think about it. But what are those others doing there?

4. If you remember, there was a 2D component of a lady there at the start of the modeling process to help us visualize scale. You deleted her pretty quick. But the materials that made up her clothing have remained in your SketchUp model.

5. Go to **Window ¦ Model Info** and click on the **Statistics** option. You'll see here a list of what's in your model. More about this in a moment. For now, notice there's a total of 9 materials listed.

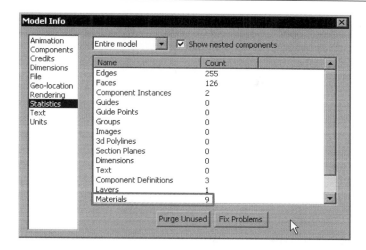

6. Now click on **Purge Unused**. The **Materials** count reduces to **1**, and your **Materials Pallet** now only shows your texture material. Phew. The world's as it should be again!

7. Click on the **Paintbucket** tool and click on the top face of the left hand member. It's not pretty is it? SketchUp is applying your texture in a random way onto this face. Go to **Edit ¦ Undo Paint**.

8. In the **Materials Pallet**, click on the **Sample Paint** tool which looks like an eye dropper. Click on the top face on one of the planks. Alternatively, with the Paint bucket tool still in use, hold *Alt* (Windows) or *Command* (Mac) to access the eye dropper.

9. Now here's the single click magic. Click on the top face of the left hand member again. Notice the difference? You now have texture, shading and shadow exactly where it should be.

This is because when CGTextures.com took the photograph for the texture you're using, the object they captured has already had texture, shading and shadow. You're simply recreating what already existed in the real world.

Have you noticed that your extruded member is too wide or too narrow for the texture? That's expected, because you just made it a random size that looked about right. All you need to do now is move the right hand face a little to line up with the wood edge in the texture.

10. Select the Push/Pull tool and click on the right-hand side face of the member. Move this face until its edge lines up with the edge in the texture.

11. Repeat steps 8-10 for the other two members.

12. Click on the **Top** view icon. You should see the following. Good, isn't it?

13. To complete the texturing you just have a few finishing touches to make. Select the **Paint Bucket** again, click on your texture in the Materials Pallet, and apply the material to the end of one of the cross members.

14. Click on the **Right** view icon.

15. Right click on the face and select **Texture ¦ Position**. Use the mouse to drag the texture so that one of the wood ends covers the face, as shown below.

16. As you can see, the texture needs to be reduced in size by over a half. Do this now by finding the Green pin and dragging it to the left until the wood end texture fits. It will help if you also drag the texture so that the red-colored pin is to the bottom left of the pallet.

17. Now, right-click and select **Done**.

18. To avoid having to re-scale the texture again for the other wood ends, use the **Sample Paint** tool and apply the texture to the other two faces.

19. Now, when you use **Texture ¦ Position** on these faces there's nothing else to do except move the other two wood end textures into place. You should have something like the following.

Have a go hero

Sample one of these wood ends and apply the material to the other ends of the timber members, but for these next three, try out some more of the options within **Texture ¦ Position**. You can **rotate, scale,** and **move** the three wood ends to provide variations on the other three ends. Try to use each of the four colored pins to see what each one does.

When you've done that, continue with the rest of the tutorial.

Time for action – recycling textures for use on non-vital faces

You really only prepared textures for the top of the pallet and wood ends. Should you now go back and make more textures for the rest? Why should you, if you can get away with recycling what you've got? Here's how to use plain areas of the timber texture within your existing texture, to complete the model.

1. Triple click each of the three members in turn, right-click and select **Group**.

2. Now go to **View ¦ Component Edit ¦ Hide rest of model**. This means when you edit any of these groups, you'll only see that group and nothing else. This is going to help you finish the more inaccessible bits of texturing.

3. Double-click on the left-hand side member to edit it. Select the **Paint Bucket** tool and paint the texture. Did you notice it's the wrong scale? Undo this, and click on the texture in the Materials Pallet. This resets it back to its original scale.

4. Now apply the texture again. Right-click and go to **Texture ¦ Position**. Move one of the timber planks over the face until it's covered, as you can see in the following screenshot.

5. Now, do this for each face that has no texture yet. Remember that the bottom planks are a **Component** copy of the upper planks, so there's no need to do those.

6. Now to texture the planks' ends. Select the first face and start moving the texture as before. Line up one of the long planks so that it covers *all* the planks' ends. See the next screenshot. The plank texture is highlighted with a rectangle.

7. Now when you sample this face, you can paint the texture to each of the other planks' ends, and they will pick up the texture position you just created.

8. You're finished texturing! Select the bottom plank component, right click and select **Make Unique**. Delete all but the side and middle planks.

9. Go to **Camera ¦ Perspective** to switch on a more pleasing view. Your completed pallet should now look something like the one below.

What Just Happened?

You've learned how to manipulate your basic texture in lots of ways to texture the faces contained in your model. You've used the **Sample** function to copy and reuse texture placement from one face to another. You've also recycled areas of timber in the same texture to provide textures for all the other timber faces that didn't have specific textures made for them. This way, you've been able to produce a model that has only one texture associated with it.

 You can find the example file of this completed model in the download pack named Chapter03_pallet_MASTER.skp.

Now, it's time to prepare your model for use in games. Save your project, then go to **File ¦ Save As** to save a separate file. Name it pallet_gameready.

Preparing for game use

Even though the model already looks complete, there are a few things you need to do to prepare it for game use. It's a list that's the same for any asset you create from now on. Here's what you need to do:

- Remove the hidden geometry and layers
- Remove unseen faces
- Explode geometry to remove groups and components
- Purge unused materials
- Check if all faces are facing outward
- Move files and textures into correct folders
- Compress or resize textures
- Save in a recognized format

It's really quick to do, and well worth the time getting right. If you start distributing assets with any of these left undone, you will pay the price by being labeled an amateur.

Hidden geometry and layers

First of all, check that you haven't hidden anything and that all layers are visible. As a rule I never use layers in SketchUp, but if you have used layers then you need to check there's nothing on a hidden layer that you have forgotten about.

1. Go to **View ¦ Hidden Geometry**.
2. If anything appears, right click on it and select **Unhide**.
3. Go to **Window ¦ Layers**. Check if all layers have a check in the **Visible** field.
4. If there is more than one Layer, go to **Edit ¦ Select All**. Then right-click and select **Entity Info**. Select **Layer0**. If you have components in your model, you will have to repeat this step for each unique component.

Removing unseen faces

There are parts of your model that have faces overlapping other faces. That's bad. How will the game engine know which to display? We're going to remove them.

1. Select the three cross members by holding down *Shift* when you click on them. Right-click and select **Explode**.
2. Now right-click again and select **Intersect Faces ¦ With Model**.
3. Select all the top and bottom plank components, right-click and select **Hide**.

4. Select and delete all the faces that have a plank going over the top. Do the same with the bottom.

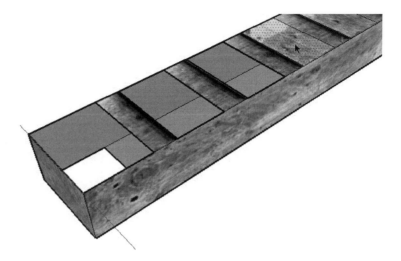

5. Go to **Window ¦ Outliner,** and in the **Outliner Pallet** select the two **pallet_boards** components and select **Unhide** from the right click menu.

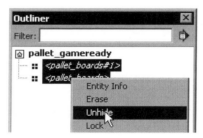

6. Double click to edit the top component. Pull a box all round the geometry with the **Select** tool to select all geometry, then right click and select **Intersect Faces ¦ With Model**.

7. This creates faces at all the points where the planks intersect the cross members. Delete all the overlapping faces again as shown:

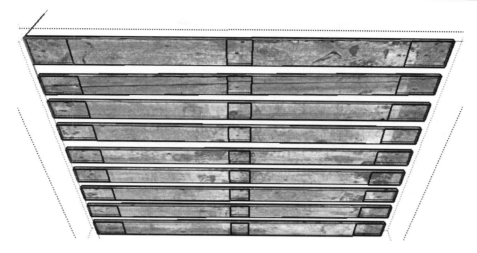

8. Repeat with the bottom component, too.

9. When you're done the whole thing looks exactly the same as before, but now you only have faces where they need to be.

Exploding geometry

Exploding geometry has nothing to do with demolishing the school math building. It's simply where you take geometry that used to be in groups and components and make it just geometry again. You do this because in games it's cleaner to have one single mesh if you can.

Save your model

Before you do anything drastic like the step below, remember to save your model. It's good, while learning, to have several versions of your model saved at intervals while you are working, so that you can go back to a previous version if you get yourself stuck. You can simply label your models with successive numbers in the filename.

Select the whole model (**Edit ¦ Select All**), right-click and select **Explode**.

Purging unused geometry and materials

This part is really easy - you already did it once earlier in the chapter. Go to **Window ¦ Model Info ¦ Statistics** and click on **Purge Unused**.

Checking the face orientation

Click the **Monochrome** faces icon. All faces should show up in light grey. If there are any blue faces, right-click on them and select **Reverse Faces**. If you don't do this, faces may be invisible in the game engine.

Click the **Shaded with Textures** button to return to your normal textured view.

Compressing and resizing textures

You remember you saved several versions of your texture? Now's the time to see whether a smaller texture will look ok on this asset. If it does, you will make your game go faster because of it.

1. In the Materials Pallet click on the **Edit** tab. This provides details of the material you've been using.

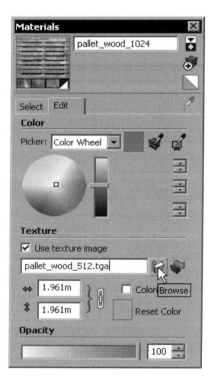

2. Click on **Browse** and navigate to your texture called `pallet_wood_512.tga`

3. Click on **Open**. The new texture will take the place of the old one. Do you see any difference?

4. Since there's no noticeable loss of quality with the lower resolution texture, let's stick with that one instead.

Checking in-game

It is not guaranteed that the texture processing in SketchUp is identical to the one used in a game engine. The model view in SketchUp can only serve as a guide. If you have a particular game application in mind, you can do this check in the game engine instead and see the results more accurately. If you are creating an asset to be used more generally, as is the case here, this technique is good enough.

Saving for game use

Now it's time to save the model and texture in their own folder. Go to **File ¦ Save As** and create a folder called `pallet_gameready`. Save your SketchUp model in there. Also move your 512-pixel texture into that folder. Repeat steps 1-3 above to reattach this new texture to the SketchUp model. This step is necessary to redefine the path for the new `pallet_gameready` folder.

If you have SketchUp Pro version, go to **File ¦ Export** and select the .fbx format. You could also choose some other well-known formats such as **3DS** and **OBJ** to allow your asset to be imported to the greatest variety of game engines. Unity uses .fbx so that's all we need for now. If you have the free version of SketchUp, select **Collada**. You will find out how to convert this to FBX in *Chapter 6, Importing to a Professional Game Application: Unity 3D*.

Summary

Now that you've completed this chapter, you are most of the way to becoming a quality asset creator. If you failed some of the steps, don't worry about it. It will all come clear as we go on. You can always come back and try it again later.

The techniques you have learned in this chapter are the basis of great modeling in SketchUp. It's a focussed approach with a quality outcome. Don't forget to download the download pack from Packt's site and compare your asset to the final file in Chapter 4's folder, named `Chapter4_pallet_gameready.skp`.

In this chapter, we covered:

- Some of the main SketchUp modeling and editing tools
- Creating groups and components for quick modeling
- The main texturing techniques for ultra realistic textures
- How to model from a texture
- Making varied use of the same texture
- How to prepare "game-ready" models
- How to export your file

I hope you enjoyed yourself. You should be proud of what you've achieved. In the next chapter, you're going to apply these skills to game level design.

5
Game Levels in SketchUp

3D games come in many varieties. First of all, they vary in the way they display the game world, either as a top-down view (a bit like a board game), or from the side similar to a platform game, or from eye-level.

Then there's how they control the way you follow your game character. Do you simply see through the eyes of your character and see what they see? Or, is your character in front of you, and your point of view remains behind them? Maybe the scene in front of you is static and only changes screen by screen. Maybe you are looking down like a god and the scene only scrolls to the North, South, East or West when your character gets near the edge.

Whichever different game configurations you could choose, the same basic element can be found in every one of them--The Level. A level is a section or a stage in the game. When you design your game, you break it up into levels, because this will keep you from having to think of the whole game at once. For example, you may be creating an adventure game taking part throughout the continent of South America. You may break your game up into levels such as The Airport, The Hotel, The Mayan Village, The Jungle, and so on. Each of these may still be too big, so you may choose to divide them up further into sub-levels, which are more focused on a particular goal within the main level. Within the airport level, you may have five sub-levels based on progressing through parts of the airport until you reach the plane, or from the plane to the taxi.

A level is a discrete area within your game world. In games such as the adventure game I have described, the levels may be quite large and unwieldy, in others, such as those with huge maps to explore, they become just too big to handle. For this reason when you design your games, you will almost always break up the levels into further chunks. The best way of thinking about this is to take the analogy of a chess board. The chess board is the game world, which has just one level, but that level is broken up into squares. Each square has a reference, A4 or F1, so that we all know where it is. The chess pieces are the players or non-player characters that move around in that level. Now, in your game you can break up your levels into squares, too. Each square will be an element of the game level. When you create many squares, your game level will be complete.

Here is the game square you will be creating in this book:

If this game had a specific task carried out in the square (as shown in the previous screenshot) before allowing you to move to the next square, this would be a game level in itself. If not, you would add other squares to it until your whole level, or game world, is complete.

Level creation is an art. In order to create a masterpiece, you need all the right tools at your disposal. You've already encountered SketchUp and GIMP. In the previous two chapters, you became proficient with these tools. In this chapter, you'll really start to see their potential as you whiz through creating a small level in a single chapter.

When you have finished this chapter, you'll have the basic level shown here. This is called a "plate", and it's the basic floor level area that you will add assets to. Assets are things like trees, plants, fences, and buildings.

In this chapter, you will:

1. Create a basic floor plate (terrain) with all textures present
2. Stamp flat road geometry onto your plate
3. Create the hilly terrains with SketchUp **Sandbox** tools
4. Add shadows to simulate depth
5. Create seamless and tile-able textures

Sketching out the level

To start with, you need some idea of what your level will look like. In a game development environment, you will usually be given this "look" by your art director. As an asset artist or level designer, you will take their specifications and drawings, and turn them into a 3D reality. The level designer will already have thought about game-play, the level of difficulty, the challenges to be contained in the level, overall look and feel, and perhaps the lighting quality and sound. You will also have parameters to stick to within the whole game production:

- Is the game set in the real world or fantasy or sci-fi?
- What's the date?
- Are graphics cartoony, realistic, edgy, dreamlike, happy, or dark?
- How quickly should the graphics render: low or high detail?

As well as many more.

Your job as a game artist, level designer, or asset modeler is to stay rigidly within the parameters that you have been given and, having done that, to shine through with your incredible artistic and modeling talent.

This chapter will show you some of the basics of level modeling and texturing—enough to get you going, and start you off building games for your portfolio or to include it in your own game. Game companies tell us that it's better to have a few small and perfectly executed examples in your portfolio than many large unfinished or below-par examples. So, take your own time on this one, and add some of your own artistic flourishes as you go on, but stay within the basic tutorial steps I've explained to you.

Do game artists need art degrees?

When researching this book I looked at lot of job adverts to see what requirements gaming companies look for in 3D modelers. One thing that surprised me was that all modelers seemed to be called artists. Now, this may be my opinion, but I don't think that a modeler or texture creator always needs to be that artistic. Rather, it depends on the game. Most 3D games have a story that's based in the real world, and in a recognizable period of history that is well documented for us, such as the Roman times or the Wild West. Creating assets and levels for these worlds don't require high artistic ability to create objects from scratch—from your imagination—because you can either go and see the object outside your own window, or look it up in a book or on the Web. We're not recreating the wheel here. It is, however, necessary in many cases to have a good appreciation of light, color, and form—subjects which you can always read up by yourself or you can take an introductory art or photography class.

When you're considering a career as a 3D artist for a game or film, don't be put off by the job title. Go for the roles you're most comfortable with. If you have a past experience in certain areas through work or hobbies, why not lean towards those areas? Here are some broad categories where similar styles of modeling can be used for each item within the category:

- Buildings, architecture, scenery items, street furniture, and interior assets
- Cars, aircraft, spacecraft, robots, and military vehicles
- Characters, monsters, organic forms and scenery, and clothing
- Objects, weapons, tools, and equipment

The more you have studied, played, or worked in the areas touching the previously described categories, the more natural you will be at recreating them for games. For example, many architects, product designers, engineers, and fashion designers go into game asset and level designing. Remember to choose what you're good at already, and stick to it until you're comfortable venturing into other areas.

Have a go hero – simple concept sketching in SketchUp

When it comes to level concept design don't worry if, like me, you're more comfortable drawing with a pen and ruler than a stick of charcoal. The idea here is to get your design intention down on paper. When you do this it has to be quick and fluid. No masterpieces, please. When you do concept work you must do it mostly within your minds eye, and then try to transfer it to paper before your mind gets too far ahead of you. Give this a go now. It doesn't matter what you end up with, good or bad.

[This tutorial assumes you want to create a first person exploration style game, which is what we will be making in this book.]

1. Grab a blank piece of paper, as large as possible.

2. Draw a circle at the start, then a rectangle for the end of the level. Label these A and Z.

3. You now need to plot a route through the piece of paper from A, to Z. Simple as that.

4. Draw your character at A, roughly to scale.

5. Draw in some scenery, props within the character's vision that will give some immediate sense of being somewhere.

6. Do the same at the Z location. It should be a place worth getting to.

7. Now the rest of your job is to put obstacles in the way of your character to impede them from getting to Z. These may be physical obstacles as well as mental obstacles. Fundamentally, a game is about overcoming challenges. It is the skill of the level designer to make this fun, frustrating, and interesting; just right to keep players hooked.

8. Once you've drawn these in, the next thing you need is a way to keep your character from wandering off where you don't want them to go. In other words, places you haven't modeled in detail!

9. Think up a device for doing this. Fences? Blind alleys? Impenetrable forests? Even other characters that stop your character getting away. Even the most open and explorable game worlds have some boundaries somewhere.

10. Now, indicate if you will be having distant scenery objects to add to the realism and finish off the scene.

11. Taking your sketch as a basis, open SketchUp and use basic modeling with the pencil tool, rectangle tool, and **Push/Pull** tool to create a 3D mock up.

12. Use the origin, where the initial 2D character is when you open SketchUp, as the starting position, and to give you an idea of scale.

Here's what you might have mocked up for the level you're now going to create. As you can see, it's roughly to scale, but not artistic, not beautiful, and most definitely not impressive. However, if you don't go through the basic planning process, you will end up modeling things you later find you don't need. Also, with a simple mock up like this, you can discuss various issues with other members of your team. In a similar way, this is the image I sent my editor when we were deciding what to include for this book.

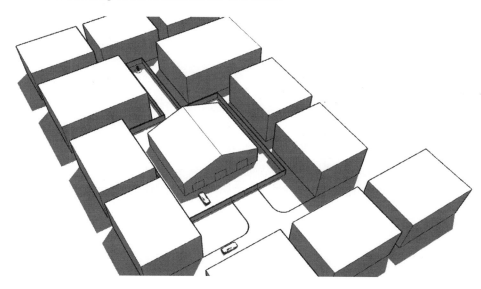

Time for action – setting up the terrain grid and plan

Now that your concept design is documented, save that file for reference later, and then start a new one in order to begin work on your actual game level. You will begin by drawing out your plan in 2D in SketchUp, based on your mock up. You'll use this as a basis for your 3D terrains, buildings, and scenery assets:

1. Open a new project in SketchUp. Select the **Engineering – Meters** template. Save the file as `Level_Master.skp`.

2. Go to **Camera ¦ Parallel Projection.**

3. Select the **Top** view button if you're not already there. You now see a completely flat 2D working area.

4. Select the **Rectangle** tool. Click on the **Origin** point and draw a rectangle to the upper right-hand side. Click again.

5. Now type in **100,100** and hit *Enter*. You now have a rectangle of 100 square meters.

6. Right-click on the face of the rectangle and select **Reverse Face.**

7. Click on the **Zoom Extents** button.

8. This is the extent of your map square, like the square on your chess board. Double-click on the rectangle, right click and select **Make Component.** Enter the name `Map_Base_2D`. Make sure **Replace selection with component** is ticked. Now click on **Create.**

9. Go to **Window ¦ Preferences ¦ Extensions** and make sure **Sandbox Tools** is checked. Now enable the toolbar by going to **View ¦ Toolbars ¦ Sandbox.**

10. Click on the **From Scratch** button. Now type in **2** and hit *Enter*.

11. Click at the bottom left-hand side of your rectangle and then at the top left-hand side. Move to the right-hand side and click on the top right corner.

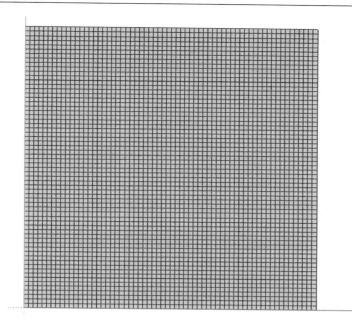

12. You're right! It's not that interesting yet! Use the middle mouse button to orbit the view, so you can see the square in 3D.

13. From the **Outliner**, select the component called **Map_Base_2D**. Now, use the **Move** tool to move it up along the blue axis out of the way, say 30 or 40 meters.

14. Select your grid, right click and select **Flip Along ¦ Group's Blue**.

What just happened?

You now have your grid and flat rectangle on top of each other. The grid will form your final terrain. The flat rectangle will contain only the plan's layout drawing. The reason you have placed a copy of it over the grid is because you will later be able to project geometry from it into your terrain. Your grid is 100x100 square meters, made up of a 50m tall by 50m wide grid of 2 squares. The reason you flipped the grid over is because the blue side was at the uppermost side. That's the back side, as you discovered in *Chapter 4, Wooden Pallet: Modeling*.

But why do you need to have a grid of squares in the first place? The grid is there so that you can create a 3D terrain. Each of the points on this grid will be raised or lowered as you wish, to create a mountainous, undulating, hilly, or rough terrain. When you've finished this level, you will be able to experiment with these techniques to create terrains very, very, quickly, for example:

I made this as a quick mock up of a possible game level, using only a Google Earth image and the sandbox tools. You can see the geometry in the next image. You can see that there are quite a lot of faces (polygons) in this square. A lot of them are unnecessary because, as you can see here, many of the surfaces are quite flat or smooth and could be defined with much less geometry than is the case here. You can head to *Appendix A* to find out how reduce the number of polygons with MeshLab.

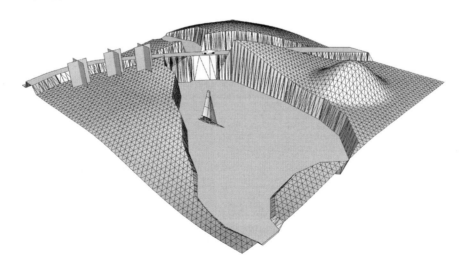

Time for action – setting up the terrain texture image

Before we go on with modeling the terrain, let's set up the texture image which you will project onto the terrain.

1. Open up GIMP and go to **File ¦ New**.

2. Type in width **2048** and height **2048** in pixels.

3. Go to **File ¦ Save As** and name the image `Map_Master.xcf`.

4. Draw something random on the image using the **Paint Brush** tool, and then go to **File ¦ Save a Copy**.

5. Save a copy of the image in PNG format named `Map_2048.png`.

6. Back in SketchUp, go to **File ¦ Import** and select **png** from the drop down list. Select the image you just saved and select **Use as Image**. Click on **Open**.

7. Select the bottom left, and then the top right of the grid rectangle. This inserts your image at the same size and location as your grid.

8. With the **Move** tool, click on the image. Hold *Ctrl* (the *Option* key on the Mac) and move up along the blue axis and click.

Awkward selection tip

If you can't get to something to select it, make use of the **Outliner**. The Outliner contains all of your Groups and Components and allows you to select them without needing to click on them. You can also right-click and use **hide / unhide** to temporarily remove groups or components that are in the way.

9. Hide the **Map_Base** component so that you can get at the first image. Select and delete the original image.

10. Unhide the **Map_Base** component. You will have the following:

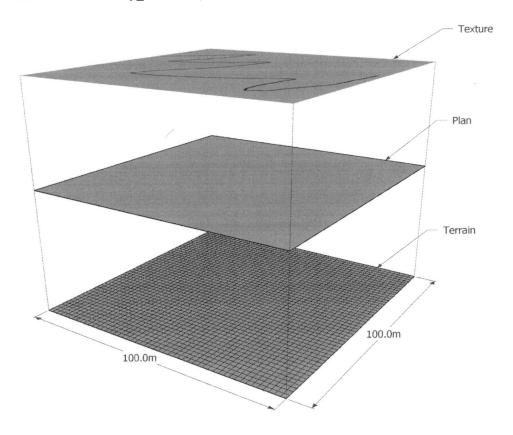

11. Right-click on the image and select **Explode**.

12. Now, in the **Materials** pallet, select the **Sample** tool and click on the image to sample it. If using a Mac machine, select the **Paint Bucket** and command **Click on the image**.

13. Press the spacebar to return to the **Select** tool. Double-click on the Map_Base component. Re-select the **Paint Bucket** tool and paint the face.

14. Finally, double-click on the original image. Right-click and select **Group**. Hide this group.

You can find this setup in the download pack under Chapter 5's code named Chapter5_Level_Master.skp

What just happened?

You have now created a master texture in GIMP. You exported a copy image and imported it into SketchUp, where you scaled and placed it exactly over the rectangle you created earlier. You now have a terrain, a 2D plan, and a texture. All of them are the same size and are lined up with each other.

Make sure you save your SketchUp file now. It's now time to rough out the game map. You can see the map as follows:

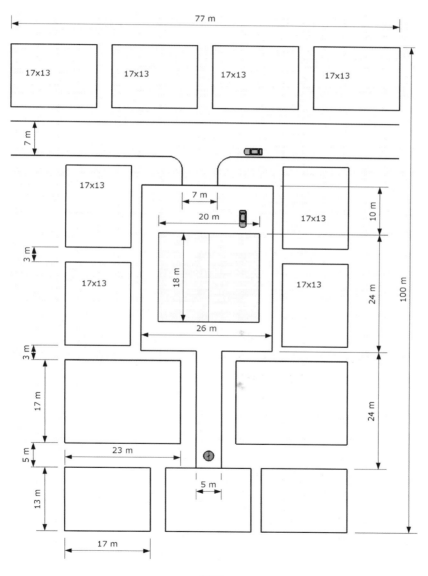

Have a go hero – creating the 2D map

Now it's your turn to put some of your new SketchUp skills into practice—the ones you learned in *Chapter 4, Wooden Pallet: Modeling*. Have a go at drawing out the plan in your SketchUp project:

1. Hit the **Top view** button and double-click on the 2D map component to get started.

2. Use the **Rectangle** and **Pencil** tool to draw the plan to the dimensions shown next. Use the **Tape Measure** tool to create offset guidelines.

3. All the rectangles are either 17x13 or 23x17, so just draw one of each and then use the **Move** tool to copy them around. Check back in *Chapter 4, Wooden Pallet: Modelling* if you need any help.

You don't need to be exact. Just get the main elements in about the same place as I've got them. Note that the plan on the previous page it is 77m wide so that it fits nicely into the page of the book. Yours will be centered on your 100m wide map. Draw the roads to the edge of the map.

If you get stuck, you can get the completed file from the download package, named Chapter5_Level_Part01.skp or take a look at the videos *Plan Construction Video 01* and *Plan Construction* Video *02*. You can open these in your web browser by going to **File ¦ Open File**.

Time for action – creating a color selection layer

1. When you're done, go to the **Materials** pallet and select a random color. Use it to fill an area of the map. Now, do this for all of the other areas too. You should choose colors that provide good contrast, and you should color similar areas (for example, all the small buildings) the same.

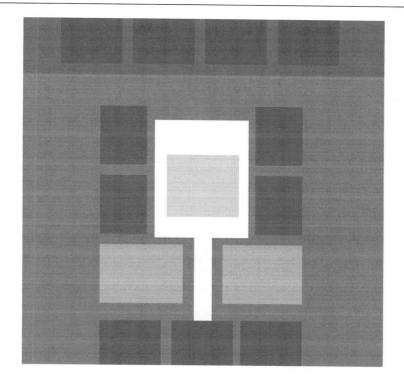

2. Make sure you're in the **Top view**, and **Perspective** is switched off.

3. Now, go to **View ¦ Edge style** and turn off **Profiles** and **Edges**.

4. Go to **File ¦ Export ¦ 2D Graphic**. Now select **PNG**.

5. Go to **Options** and input a height of *2000* and uncheck the **Anti-Alias** box.

6. Save the image as a PNG file named Map_Selection.png.

7. Open this image in GIMP. Go to **Image ¦ Autocrop Image**.

8. Now to resize the image to the same size as your master texture, go to **Image ¦ Scale Image** and type in *2048* then click on **Scale**.

9. Go to **Select ¦ All** then **Edit ¦ Copy**.

10. Open up your Map_Master.xcf file and go to **Edit ¦ Paste**.

11. Right-click in the layers pallet where it says **Floating Selection** and select **New Layer**, or go to **Layers ¦ New Layer**.

What just happened?

You now have a layer in GIMP that you can use to select any of the main areas you need to work on. Try it now by selecting the **Fuzzy Select** tool and by clicking somewhere in the image. GIMP will now only work in the part of the image you selected. Switch off the **Map Selection** layer and select the original layer in the **Layer** pallet. Use the **Bucket Fill** tool to fill that selected area full of color. Can you see how this can be used to control where you're working on the main texture?

Use *Ctrl-Z* (*Cmd-z* on the Mac OS) to undo the **Color fill**. Save your file. Let's get started on the texture for real.

The master texture

You're now all set to find the textures you want from CGtextures.com, other websites, or from your own images. You will use these to build up a master texture which you will project onto your terrain. You'll then use **Sandbox** tools to sculpt your terrain. Your terrain texture will look something like this:

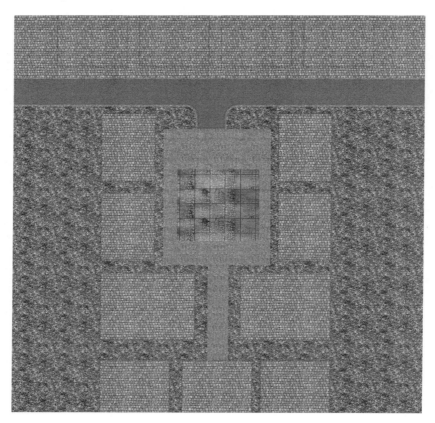

Time for action – creating a large seamless texture

The main area that your character will be walking around in is made of worn concrete. This is brought on to site in huge slabs and laid down. The idea we're trying to give here is of a worn, old, and weathered surface:

1. Go to CGTextures.com and find **ConcreteFloors0060** using the search feature. Download the small versions of image 02 and 05.

2. Open image 02 in GIMP. Select the **Crop** tool and use it to draw a box around the edges of six concrete squares as you can see here:

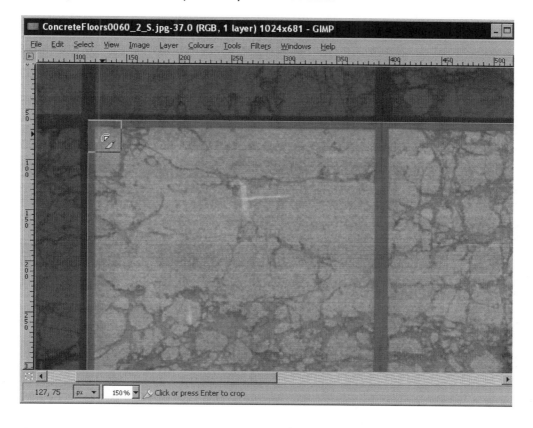

3. When you've fine-tuned the corners so that they sit in the middle of the steel edges (as shown in the screenshot), press *Enter* to complete the crop.

4. Now go to **Image ¦ Canvas Size** and de-select the chain icon.

5. Change **Pixels** to **Percent**. Now, enter **200%** in the height box.

6. Click on **Resize**. You now have six concrete slabs at the top of the image, and room for six more as shown next:

7. Go to **File ¦ Open as Layers**. Select the other texture you downloaded. This now opens in its own layer.

8. Select the **Move** tool and drag the new texture into place so that it fits below the previous one. You should have something like the one following:

Smooth mover

While you have the **Move** tool selected, you can also tap the arrow keys on your keyboard to move a layer by single pixel increments.

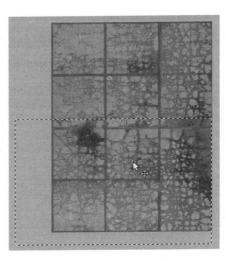

9. Click on the uppermost layer in the **Layer** pallet and right-click. Select **Add Layer Mask**. If using a Mac, go to **Layer ¦ Mask ¦ Add Layer Mask**.

10. Now select the **Paint Brush** tool and begin painting along the top edge of the layer to blend it in with the one below. Make sure the black and white foreground and background colors are selected by clicking the icon shown with an arrow in the next screenshot, and switch black to the foreground color if you need to with the little double arrow.

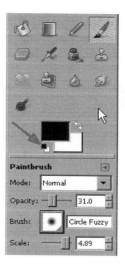

11. Now select one of the fuzzy brushes and set the scale and opacity. Opacity reduces the strength of the effect, so setting it lower will now allow you to fine-tune your blend.

12. When you're done, the one layer should be blend in seamlessly with the other. You can see the result in the following screenshot:

13. At the top is the layer mask so that you can see the simple rough edge I've created. In the middle is the mask applied to the upper layer, and below that is the finished effect. For a rough texture like this, this quick technique is usually good enough. At other times, you may need to use more brush strokes.

Time for action – creating a tiled texture

You will use this technique of blending layers together over and over again in the future. Let's move on and see whether we can get this texture to repeat seamlessly. This is called **tiling**. Tiling is useful when we have a large area to cover with the texture.

1. Go to **Layer ¦ Layer to Image Size**.

2. Save your project as a GIMP XCF file before doing the next command. Now, go to **Image ¦ Flatten image**. This removes all the layer information:

 Before transforming a layer as per the next step, you will need an image that is an even number of pixels, wide and high. If your image is not, use **Image ¦ Canvas Size** to take off a row of pixels where needed. Remember to uncheck the chain icon so that the height and width don't change together.

3. Go to **Layer ¦ Transform ¦ Offset**. Click on the button that says **Offset by X/2, Y/2**. Now click on **Offset**.

4. Everything should look absolutely fine, apart from a black strip down the middle. It's there because the second texture didn't quite fit, and left a gap at the edge. No problem!

5. Select the clone tool. Hold down *Ctrl (Cmd on Mac)* and click at the corner of the steel frame as you can see in the following screenshot:

6. Now, release the *Ctrl (or Cmd)* button and move to the right-hand side. Begin painting from there (see the next screenshot):

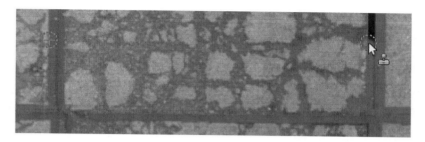

7. This clones the area on the left over the area on the right. The left-hand part of the clone tool moves along with your brush. Do this all the way up. As you paint further up, you may need to release the mouse button. If you do this the clone tool will start back at the spot you placed it when you released the *Ctrl (or Cmd)* button. You may need to find another spot and continue from there.

8. You've now cloned over the empty area of the image. The rest of the texture looks fine, so let's tile it now.

9. Save the image as a new file into your texture library so that you can use it again and again. Now you need to tile it for the map.

Do the math

Our map has around 2000 pixels per side, which accounts for 100 meters. So, 2000/100 is 20, telling us that 1 meter is equivalent to 20 pixels on our image. Or in other words, 1 pixel is 50mm in the real world.

10. Three of these concrete slabs should amount to about 10m in the real world, so let's resize the image to 200 pixels wide (because 10 meters times 20 pixels equals 200).

11. When you've done that, go to **Filters ¦ Map ¦ Tile** and deselect the chain and type in 2048 in width and height.

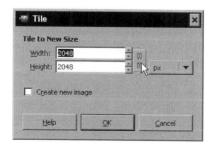

12. Deselect **Create new image** and click **OK**. The image is tiled to form a texture of the same size as your map texture. **Use Filters ┊ Enhance ┊ Unsharp Mask** now if you wish.

13. Use **Colours ┊ Auto ┊ White balance** to correct the contrast.

What just happened?

You've just taken another giant leap forward in your game art skills. You now know how to create seamlessly tiled textures, and how to repeat them within GIMP to cover any given size of image. You started with the basic textures from the CGTextures store and added two of them together. You then masked off part of the overlapping image to blend it into the image below. This is the main technique you will need for the creation of any texture on GIMP, and will serve you well for years to come. Using **Layers** with **Masks** is also the key to productivity in texturing, and will open the door to many other skills and techniques.

You have learned how to heal an image by **Cloning** areas of the image to somewhere else.

Now it's time to introduce this tile-able texture to our main map image.

Time for action – filling selected areas with textures

1. Go to **Select ┊ All** and then **Edit ┊ Copy**.

2. Switch to your `Map_Master` project and go to **Edit ┊ Paste**.

3. Right-click your pasted item in the **Layer Pallet** and select **New Layer**.

4. You now have three layers. Label them as shown next by right-clicking and selecting **Edit Layer Attributes**.

5. You can turn the selection layer on or off at any time by clicking the eye icon. This layer will not contribute to your final image, but you will use it to select parts of it.

6. Make sure the selection layer is current by clicking it in the Layer pallet. Click the **Fuzzy Select tool** and select the area inside the industrial building at the center of the image.

7. Now hide the selection layer. Right-click on the **Concrete Floor** layer and select **Add Layer Mask**.

8. Select the button next to **Selection**, then click **Add**. You will now have the texture confined to the floor of the industrial building, as shown here.

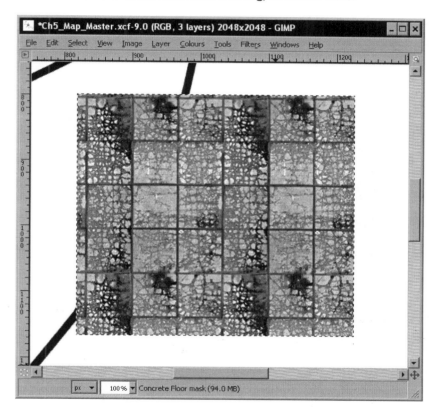

What just happened?

You've used the selection layer to control where your texture was placed. The concrete floor is now visible only within the boundaries of the area you created when you drew your 2D map. Good, isn't it?

You're going to do exactly the same with all the other textures you need, but all the rest will already be tile-able straight from CGTextures.com. This will be the easiest paint by numbers drawing you ever did, trust me!

I'll start you off with the first one, and then you can complete the rest by yourself. Let's start by downloading all the textures you'll need.

Time for action – using tileable textures from the Internet

1. Go to CGTextures.com and select **Nature ¦ Grass** from the left-hand menu. Select any of these that say "Tiled" in the title.

2. Download a small version of any of the tiled images. Usually these are shown first in the list of thumbnails.

3. Do the same with **Concrete ¦ Floors** and download any small tiled image you like. Get one that looks like it could be from an industrial yard.

4. Now you need a road surface. Try a search for *asphalt* or *tarmac*. Download a tiled one.

5. Finish off with a paved or cobbled street texture.

Have a go hero – selecting and texturing

Now it's your turn. Open up a texture in GIMP. Work out roughly how large this texture would be in real life. Take 20 pixels per meter and resize the image to the correct number of pixels. Use the quick tile filter as you've learned, use some color or contrast adjustments if you want, and create a selection mask. Easy as that!

Multiple selections
You can make multiple selections with the **Fuzzy Select Tool** by holding the *Ctrl (or Cmd on Mac)* key.

You can use the final image shown earlier in the chapter to check what goes where. Remember, this doesn't have to be perfect at this stage. It's about learning. In addition, any of your textures can easily be replaced later if you wish to by pasting into the layer you created. Working this way gives you a template in GIMP that you can keep coming back to whenever you wish to make a visual change in your game level.

Naming layers

Naming your layers as you create them saves a lot of frustration later. You will be able to see instantly which layer you need, even if you have tens of layers that all look the same.

Some nifty texture tweaks

The beautiful thing about texturing in this way is that all the textures are available at any location in the map. The only thing controlling where they're visible is the masks you created. Unmasking any area will allow the texture to shine through.

Time for action – creating a roadside kerb

1. In the **Layer** pallet, make sure the concrete road texture is above the asphalt road texture in the list.

2. Switch on the **Selection Layer**. Use the **Fuzzy Select Tool** to select the road.

3. Now go to **Select ¦ Border**. Enter **5** in the box and click on **OK**.

4. In the Layer Pallet, switch off the selection layer. Now, select the layer with your concrete texture on it. Select the mask next to it in order to start editing the mask.

5. Switch the foreground and background colors so that you have white in the foreground (you learned how to do this when you were blending together your two concrete tile floor textures).

6. Now select the **Bucket fill** tool and click inside your selection. You can see the result here:

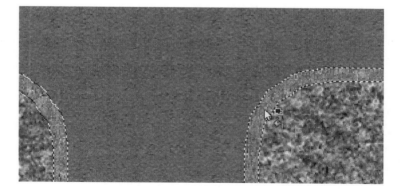

7. Now, to create some shadow at the edge of the road and roadside curb.

8. Select the road again in the same way as before. Now go to **Select ¦ Shrink**. Input *5* and click **OK**.

9. Make a new Layer by clicking the **New Layer** icon at the bottom of the Layer Pallet. Select **Transparency** and enter a **Layer name**. Click **OK**.

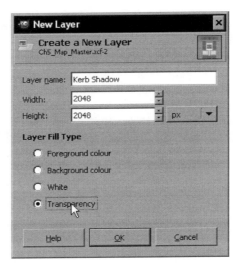

10. Move the layer to the top of the list by using the little green arrows at the bottom of the **Layer** pallet.

11. Select the **Fuzzy Select** tool and click on the **Add to current selection** button as shown next:

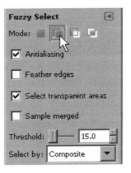

12. Select each of the rectangles on the selection layer which represent buildings.

13. Make sure black is your foreground color. Select the new layer. Now go to **Edit ¦ Stroke Selection**.

14. Select **Stroke Line**, with a **Line Width** of **4**, and select **Solid Colour**.

15. Now click on **Stroke**. A thick black line will appear along the line of all your selections. This will depict the area near buildings and roads that collects dirt and grime, also an element of shadow.

16. Make this look more real now by blurring the line. First remove your selection by going to **Select ¦ None**.

17. Go to **Filters ¦ Blur ¦ Gaussian Blur**. Leave the settings as default (5 pixels) and select **OK**.

18. Now reduce **Layer opacity** to *30%*. You can see the effect, subtle but important, in the next image:

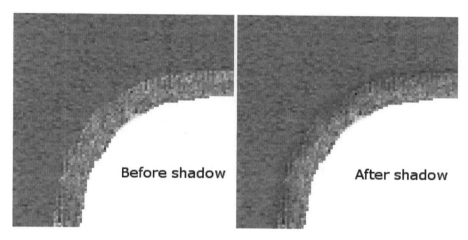

Before shadow   After shadow

What just happened?

You just learned how to create and manipulate selections in GIMP to add shadow or fill areas with texture. The shadow/dirt effect is subtle but important, as you will now see in your map texture. It has more feeling of depth, doesn't it?

Time for action – removing white edges

Selecting areas with the **Fuzzy Select tool** is not a fine art. You will have been left with some white edges between areas of texture.

1. In GIMP, select the **Cobbles** layer in the **Layer** pallet. Right-click and select **Mask to Selection**.

2. Go to **Select ¦ Grow** and input **1** into the box, and then click on **OK**.

3. Make sure your **Layer Mask** is selected. Go to the **Bucket Fill** tool.

4. Select the **Fill Whole Selection** button as shown in the following screenshot, and click in the selected area.

What just happened?

You expanded your selection area by a single pixel and then modified the layer mask to include the new selection area. This meant that any white lines at the edges of the cobbled areas were removed. You can repeat this now for any other affected areas.

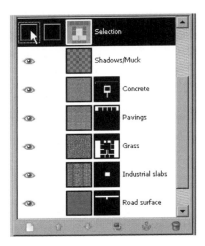

Your layer stack should now look a bit like this. The way you have it set up means that you can make changes any time without destroying any other part of the image. Using layers means you're completely safe to experiment. If you don't like the result of something, drag the layer to the trash can. Simple as that!

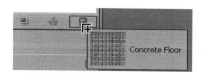

 You can get this GIMP file from the download pack called `Chapter5stage01.xcf`.

The rest of the feeling of depth will be created with actual depth, modeling the terrain itself. This is probably the most fun part of the whole modeling process, so let's leave texturing for now and craft some landscapes! Save a copy of your map texture by going to **File ¦ Save a Copy** and overwrite the `MapMaster.png` you created earlier. Now, save your GIMP project and get out of there. It's high time we got back to working within SketchUp!

Modeling terrain with Sandbox tools

Back in SketchUp, you can now start to create the actual terrain that will be imported into your game. The texture is a flat object. You will now alter the height of the terrain to create slopes, walls, and hills, as they would be in real life.

 You can use the file named `Chapter5_Level_Part01.skp` from the download pack for this exercise.

Time for action – adding height to a flat terrain

1. Open your SketchUp file and go to the **Materials** pallet. Select the Home icon and then the `MapMaster` texture.

2. Click on the **Edit** tab. Now, click on the **Browse** icon next to the texture filename and re-load your `MapMaster.png` image.

3. If your edges are still switched off, switch them back on now (**View ¦ Edge Style**).

4. You're now ready to start crafting your terrain with **Sandbox** tool. Make this possible by selecting both the base and terrain components and selecting **Explode** from the right-click menu.

5. Press the spacebar to get to selection mode and click in a blank area of the screen to deselect everything.

6. Now, click on the **Smoove** tool, type **40** and press *Enter*. This gives you a broad brush to work with.

7. Click on the terrain. Move the mouse up and down to raise or lower the terrain, as you can see in the following screenshot:

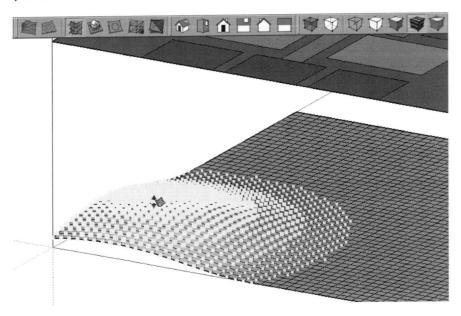

8. Click when you're done. You can undo this modification with *Ctrl-Z* (*Cmd-z* on Mac OS).

9. Do this a few times over the terrain to get the rough geometry you want. Here's mine!

10. You can now add finer undulations by reducing the radius of the **Smoove** tool. Click on the tool again, type in **20** and press *Enter*.

11. Make some adjustments with this. Then try with **10**.

12. This is mine so far. You can do it completely differently if you like.

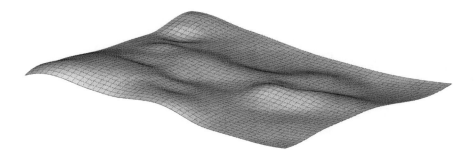

13. You can also select lines or areas of the grid directly and then *smoove* them. Go to the **Top** view, and from there, select a square of edges as shown in the following screenshot. You may need to hide the texture and plan first.

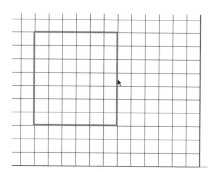

14. Now click the **smoove** tool, type in *5* and *Enter*.

15. Orbit the view. Click and move up as shown next:

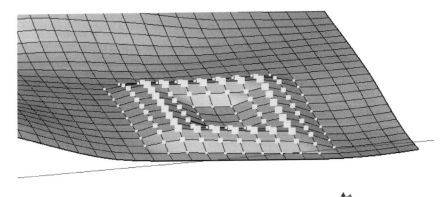

What just happened?

You've just created some random terrain using one of the **Sandbox** tools, **Smoove**. Here, you've learned how to use it with different diameters, and also when selecting parts of the grid directly. You should now have a pleasingly undulating terrain, rather than a boring flat surface. Within the game development industry, terrains are usually created within the game engine itself, an example being the terrain tools within **Unity 3D**. But what you've now learned will give you a valuable tool for your toolbox. The reason to create a terrain this way is that this terrain can be used in *any* game engine or 3D software. As such, it is possible to create and sell terrains as assets.

> You can find the SketchUp file for the project so far in the download pack, labeled Chapter5_Level_Part02.skp.

The Stamp tool

What you have now is the base deformation. It's time to stamp some of the map geometry onto it. Just as in real life, roads and buildings are more or less level surfaces placed on un-level terrain, the same we'll do in SketchUp. The **Stamp** tool will take your 2D map geometry as a base and project it onto your terrain.

I got a bit carried away...

If your terrain is a little too over the top, you can easily tone things down a little without having to go back and repeat anything. Triple-click on your terrain and turn it into a group (Right-click and select the **Group** option). Now, select **Tools ¦ Scale**. Use the top, centre grip to squash the whole group. Then, you can right-click and **Explode**.

Time for action – stamping detail onto the terrain

1. If you hid the 2D map, unhide it now using the **Outliner** pallet. Make sure it's exploded.

2. Select the **Stamp** tool. Type *2* and press *Enter*.

3. Click on the area surrounding the industrial building. You will see a red line around the area indicating where the 2 meter offset lies.

4. Click onto your terrain, which will turn blue.

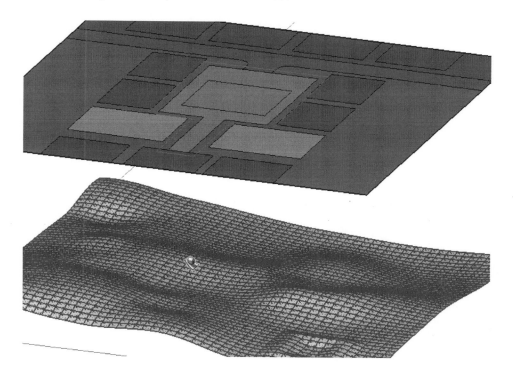

5. Wait a little while SketchUp decides how it's going to proceed. There's a progress bar at the bottom of your window.

6. You can now move the mouse up and down to stamp the selected shape onto your terrain, as you can see next:

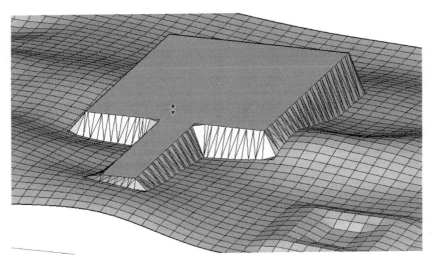

7. The 2m offset is applied as an embankment. The idea here is to make the area look like it's been built up, and cut out of the terrain. Move the mouse until you get the best balance of cut and fill, then click to exit. You can see mine from another angle here. The front is built up and the back and right side are cut in to the hillside; this is an average level of the two.

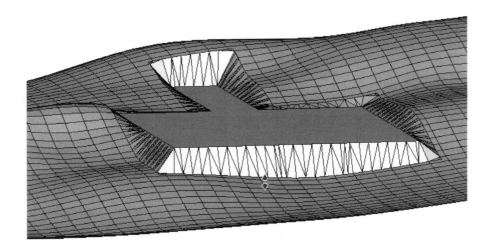

8. Now try the road in the same way like this:

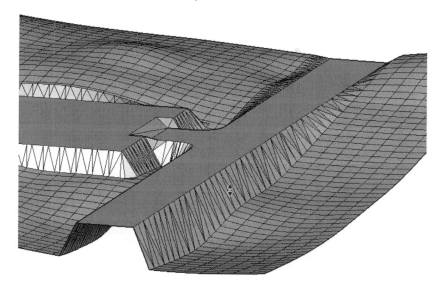

9. Now type in **1** and press *Enter*. Create a little plateau for each of the houses by the roadside, raising or lowering depending on the slope.

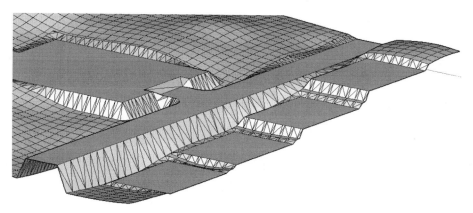

10. Use an offset of **1** for the two buildings to the left and right at the bottom of the map.

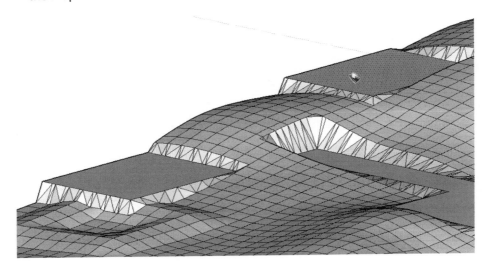

11. Use an offset of **2.5** for the building between these two, where the game character starts off. This can be turned into a feature later—steps going up to the building—where in the game's storyline the character emerges from. Try to create a 45 degree ramp, either up or down, like the one I've shown highlighted in the next screenshot:

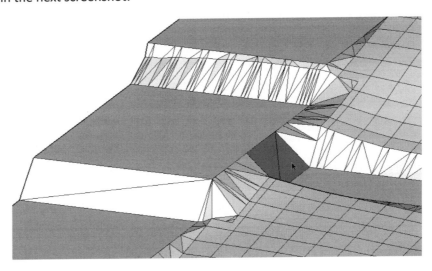

What just happened?

You should now have something like the terrain shown as in the following screenshot. Yours will differ from this because we started from different base terrains. If you don't like the one you've got, go back and have another go using different offsets. There's no right or wrong way to do this—you're just making an interesting terrain. There's an infinite number of different terrains you can make using the same 2D map, but starting with different **Smoove** base terrains and applying different stamps.

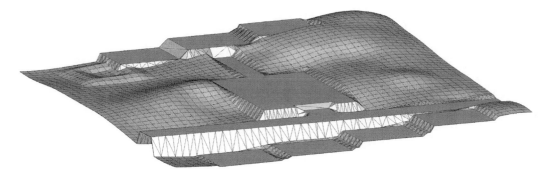

The **Stamp** tool selects geometry from a plan above or below where you want to stamp. Then, using an offset distance either side of this geometry, cuts into the terrain. The offset you entered becomes the transition zone between this new flat area and the surrounding terrain. You've used the **Stamp** tool on a hilly terrain to create a terraced effect, just as you would see in real life.

The Drape tool

Sometimes you don't want this transition effect. You don't want your terrain to look as if a landscaper's been at it with a bulldozer. The **Drape** tool allows you to retain the contours you already have, intact. Finish off your terrain now with the **Drape** tool.

Time for action – using the Drape tool

1. Press the spacebar and then select all the buildings you haven't stamped onto the terrain. Hold *Ctrl* to select multiple (*Shift* on the Mac OS).

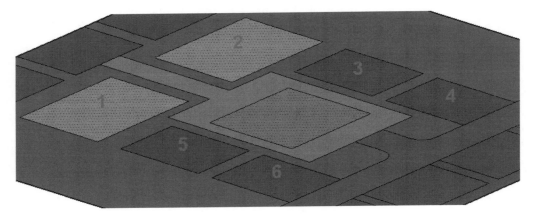

2. Now, select the **Drape** tool. Click on the terrain.

3. SketchUp stamps the seven rectangles onto the terrain without modifying anything else.

4. You're done with the 2D map for now, so turn it into a group and then hide it.

5. Select all of the terrain and turn it into a component.

What just happened?

When you used the **Drape** tool, SketchUp took the map geometry you had selected, and used it to cut edges out of the terrain. This is great because it leaves the terrain untouched around it. Defining these rectangular areas means you can later drop buildings into place, and easily delete the terrain in these spaces.

 You can find the finished terrain in the download pack, labeled `Chapter5_Terrain_Finished.skp`.

Uniting terrain geometry with texture

Now, for the fun bit where you project your texture onto the terrain to see how it looks. You have already set up your project to make this step a cinch, by lining up your texture and terrain geometry above one another.

1. In SketchUp, right-click on your terrain component and select **Soften/Smooth Edges**. Move the slider to about *33*.

2. Click on the **Soften coplanar** check box. Close the dialog by clicking the small **X button**.

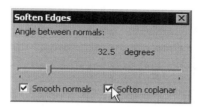

3. Unhide your **Map Texture** group and then **Explode** it.

4. Go to the **Materials** pallet and select the **Sample Paint** tool.

5. Click on the **Map Texture** to sample it. Press the spacebar. Double-click to edit the terrain.

6. Select the **Paint Bucket** tool and paste onto the terrain. If there are areas that remain white, click them too.

7. You now have a textured terrain!

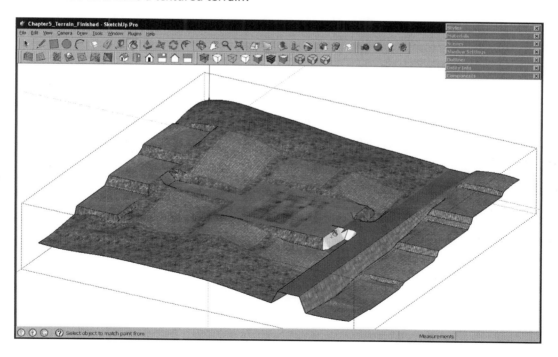

Summary

In this chapter, you have learned how to sculpt terrains in SketchUp and create a realistic terrain texture in GIMP, which you then projected onto the terrain. The big deal about this is that you now have a straightforward workflow that you can use again and again for any game project. You have learned texturing and modeling skills that will serve you in any modeling and texturing task, for any and all game objects.

To sum up, you've learned:

- How to use layers and masks in GIMP
- How to create a selection from SketchUp to use in GIMP
- How to add soft subtle shadows to give illusion of depth
- How to use the Sandbox tools in SketchUp to model terrains
- How to create seamlessly tileable textures

But listen, I've got something to whisper to you about your level, so no one else hears it.

In the next chapter, you'll get to walk around in it!!!

Sorry! I've gotten over excited with anticipation. Haven't you?

6

Importing to a Professional Game Application: Unity 3D

Maybe you were skeptical when you first looked through this book. "Will I really get to create a game level from scratch in SketchUp and get to walk around in it? Or, will I be left frustrated like I have been with other software?" Now it's time to deliver on promises. You are about to take the level *you've* made and insert it into a game application *you* can control. There's going to be no arcane wizardry you can't understand. No code. No sending you off to this or that website to work something out yourself. No sir. This is the real deal. You're about to start walking around your level, as if it were part of a real game.

No, that's not right! It *is* a real game!

In this chapter, you will:

- Export your terrain from SketchUp
- Import into Unity 3D and attach a high-resolution terrain texture
- Add collision detection
- Set up a **first person shooter** style controller
- Add lights and sun
- Walk around to admire your handiwork!

This chapter is the bridge between you as an asset and level artist in SketchUp, and the rest of the game creation process in Unity 3D. As mentioned before, Unity 3D is a game development environment with a game engine on which you can run games, then export them to different platforms, such as the Web, mobile, console, PC, and Mac. Once your level and assets are within Unity 3D, you can go on to create complete games with them.

Though you might not even need to do that.

What you get in this book is a fully explorable level that can be immediately exported and played on any computer or over the Web. For a lot of applications (real estate, for example) this is the end result you're after. Also, if you're producing a portfolio for a game or other media company, it's all you need. Game asset artists wouldn't be expected to be game coders or level designers too. It's perhaps better to stick to your role and do it well.

Exporting the level from SketchUp

So, where are we at? You produced a level plate (textured terrain) in the last chapter. You can use this, or go for the one I've included in the download pack labeled `Chapter5_Terrain_Textured.skp`. If you want to skip the export stage, I've also included a FBX file, which will import straight into Unity.

> You might have already installed Unity from *Chapter 2, Tools that Grow on Trees*. If you haven't, now's the time to do it!

Time for action – preparing a model for export

1. Open your SketchUp project and go to the **Outliner** pallet. Open it from **Window ¦ Outliner** if you need to.

2. Click on the **Details** button and select **Expand All** (see the next screenshot):

3. Only your terrain should be there. Unhide any other groups and delete them. Explode your **Terrain** group.

4. Go to **View ¦ Hidden Geometry** and then delete any geometry that now appears (possibly your map or texture image).

5. Uncheck **Hidden Geometry** now.

6. Go to **Window ¦ Model Info ¦ Statistics** and click on **Purge Unused**.

7. You now don't have anything except the terrain mesh and texture. Go to **File ¦ Save As...** and save the file in your project directory, naming it as Map_Base.

8. Now, you need to save an exported version for Unity 3D. You covered this in *Chapter 4, Wooden Pallet: Modeling*, so you should be familiar with it. Go ahead and skip this section if you want to.

What just happened?

When modeling in SketchUp you will often find it useful to hide components, groups, or even individual faces or meshes so that you can see what you are working on more easily. It's easy to forget these hidden items, so when time comes to export a model, you should perform this purging process to check for anything hidden and remove it. Not doing this may make your models behave strangely in your Game Development application. The same goes for extra materials that you may have used at some stage but then replaced. They are still there in the model unless you use the **Purge Unused** option.

Time for action – SketchUp Pro export

1. Go to **File ¦ Export ¦ 3D Model** and select the **FBX** file format.

2. Click **Options** and check the **Export Texture Maps** option and **Swap YZ coordinates**. Set **Units** to **Meters**.

3. Navigate to your **Project** folder and create a new folder named Unity_Assets inside it.

4. Save your model inside it as Map_Base.

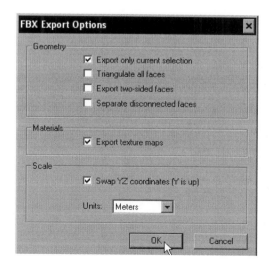

Time for action – SketchUp free export

Sketchup free version only exports to SKP (`.skp`) and Collada (`.dae`) formats. This isn't a lot of help when importing to Unity, or any other game application. There are several ways to get around this. Providing you have access to more than one computer, the easiest of these is to install an evaluation copy of **SketchUp Pro** on another computer and use it just for export. This way, the 400 minutes of free use last for ages. I've put some alternative methods in *Appendix, MakeHuman*.

1. In SketchUp (free), save your file in your project directory.

2. E-mail the file or put it on a memory stick.

3. On your second computer, start SketchUp Pro, and open your file. Now, follow the export instructions for SketchUp Pro in the previous section.

Time for action – using the free Autodesk FBX converter

There is now an easy way to convert SketchUp Collada (`.dae`) files to `.fbx` files. This has only just become possible with the 2012's release of the FBX converter. If you haven't done so already, download the Autodesk FBX converter from `http://www.autodesk.com/fbx`.

1. Export your SketchUp file as before, using the DAE format as shown next:

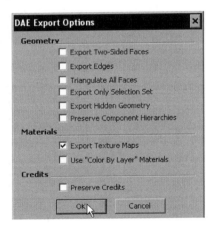

2. Open Autodesk FBX converter.

3. In the left-hand side box, click **Add...** and select your DAE file.

4. In the right-hand side box make sure **Destination Format** is set to **FBX 2012.**

5. Click on **Change destination folder** to set the destination to your game folder.

6. Now click on **Convert**. You can see the setup in the following image:

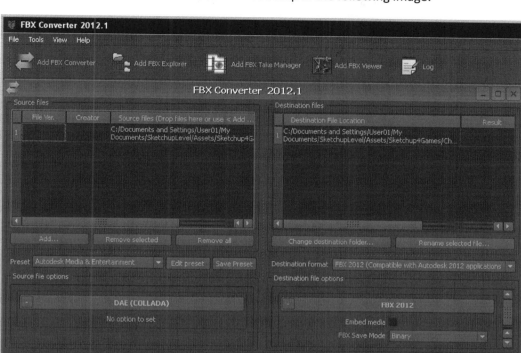

What just happened?

The newly-released 2012 version of the Autodesk FBX converter allows you to take Collada files from the Free version of SketchUp and convert them to Unity's native FBX format. This is an exciting development that many SketchUp and Unity users have been waiting for.

Importing to Unity 3D

Importing into Unity is a joy. When I say there's nothing to it, that's quite literally true. Unity automatically imports anything you save or move into its asset directory. So it's just a matter of finding where that is, and then always saving your exported files there.

The good thing about Unity is that it automatically checks for changes and updates itself with new versions of your asset files. Say you don't like the grass texture you used after all? Just change it in GIMP and export a copy of the image directly into the texture folder in Unity. Presto, the grass on your terrain changes too!

Time for action – importing your terrain in to Unity

1. Fire up your copy of Unity 3D.

2. Go to **File ¦ New Project**. Instead of where it says **New Unity Project,** type **SketchUpLevel**.

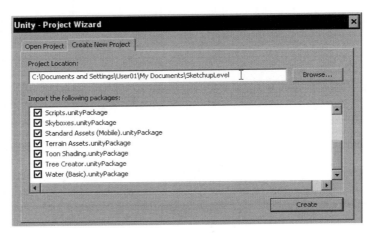

3. check all the assets you wish to import for use in your project. If you check all of them it will take a long time to load them all up. For the project in this book, you should check at least:

   ° Character controllers

   ° Sky boxes

   ° Standard assets

   ° Terrain assets

4. Click on **Create** and then wait a while for the project to install the assets.

5. Click on the small folder named **Standard Assets** shown on the right-hand side. Right-click and select **Show in Explorer** (**Reveal in Finder** on Mac OS).

6. You now have an explorer window open (Finder on Mac OS) which shows all the assets in the **Project** folder.

7. Create a new folder now named Sketchup4Games. This is where you will save all the SketchUp assets created in this book.

8. Right-click and select **Send To (desktop)**. This will give you a shortcut on your desktop to help you find this again easily. On Mac OS, you can use Command Option, and drag the folder to the Desktop.

9. Now, navigate to your `Unity_Assets` folder (where you have been saving your SketchUp assets) and copy everything to your `SketchUp4Games` folder.

10. Go back to Unity and wait for your assets to import.

11. Once you've got this set up, save your assets to your `Sketchup4Games` folder directly. They will import or update in Unity automatically.

12. **Sketchup4Games** has now appeared in your folder list in Unity. Click on the little arrow next to it.

13. The previous screenshot shows what has been imported into Unity. Click on the **Map_Base** object now, in the **Inspector** pallet, on the right-hand side of your window, and scroll down to the bottom. Here, you have a preview of your asset.

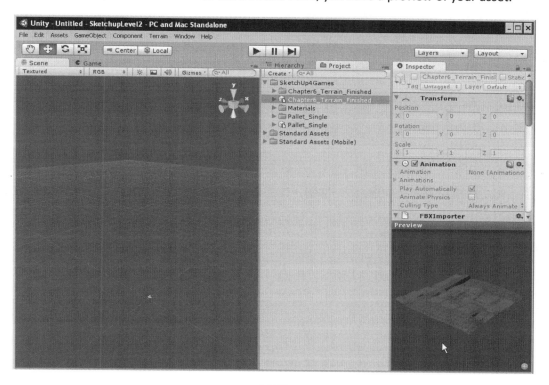

14. It looks okay, so scroll up the **Inspector** pallet until you find **FBXImporter**.

15. Enter **1** in **Scale Factor** and click on the **Generate Colliders** box. Now, scroll down and click on **Apply**.

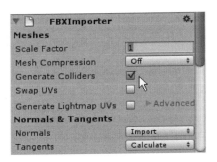

16. Now click the Map_Base icon shown in the screenshot on the last page, and drag it into the main viewing window.

17. Enter the following figures in the **Inspector** pallet:

18. Your terrain is now placed at the origin, and scaled correctly. Click on the **Hierarchy** tab.

19. Notice that this list contains all the elements within your project. Click on the **Map_Base** item now.

20. Point your cursor at the main window. Tap *F* on the keyboard. This stands for **Frame selected**, and will center your selected item in the screen.

21. Click the hand icon at the top of the screen. Use the three mouse buttons and scroll wheel to move and zoom around. Unfortunately, these controls are slightly different to SketchUp and will take a little while to get used to.

22. Finally, go to **File ¦ Save Scene** and type in Sketchup_Level. Click on **Save**.

What just happened?

You've imported your level into Unity 3D. Congratulations! From here on, creating a walk-around is a cinch. You changed some parameters to scale the mesh to retain the correct real-world dimensions you gave it in SketchUp. You set up a folder in the `Unity project` folder to hold your game level assets. Finally, you saved a `Unity Scene` file. Did you notice that this has now appeared in the project hierarchy in Unity? The **Generate Colliders** feature takes the mesh geometry and uses it to tell Unity where a physical object exists. So, in the case of your terrain, Unity will create a solid base for your character to walk on. If you didn't do this, your game characters would fall through the floor, and keep on falling forever…

That idea gives me the shivers.

Time for action – using a high-resolution terrain texture in Unity

If you zoom right in to the terrain texture you'll notice it's not a very high resolution texture. It appears to have lost some detail. In fact, this is true also of the SketchUp version. Is this right? In the **Project** tab, click on the **Map_Base ¦ Map_Master** texture (or something like `M_2048` if you used the naming scheme suggested in Chapter 3, *Wooden Pallet*: *Texture Creation*. In the **Preview** window at the bottom right-hand side, you will see the image that will look like the one following. Can you see what's wrong now?

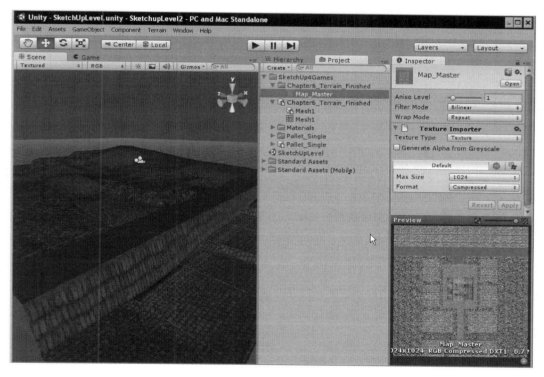

There in the bottom right-hand side is the image size, 1024! But we created a 2048x2048 image! What's happened? Actually, it's not as bad as you think, and can be easily corrected. Here's how:

1. Select the arrow next to the `Map_Base` folder and select `Map_Master`.

2. On the right-hand side, note that a **Max Size** import rule for 1024 pixels has been added. Change this now to **2048**.

3. Click on the little button shown in the top right-hand side of this screenshot and click on the **Override or Standalone** box.

4. Click **Apply** and wait for Unity to update the scene. You now have a high-resolution terrain texture; the resolution you intended to use when you made it in GIMP.

 Once you've completed the exercises in this book and you're happy with working in SketchUp, GIMP, and Unity, you can try the largest texture size allowed for the map, which is 4096x4096 pixels. You may need to increase the memory allocation in GIMP to use this image size, and if you're using an old PC, you may find it slows things down while you work on it.

What just happened?

As you know, the most important consideration when creating textured assets for games, is size. Small textures and less polygons (faces) are best for performance reasons. This is more true than ever now that 3D games are being created for tablets and phones. Unity is trying to limit the size of textures it imports to what it believes to be a sensible size for a game. We would agree with this for most things, except for this large-scale terrain texture, which we think needs to be much bigger than 1024x1024 pixels. So, we are just overruling Unity on this occasion.

Creating lights

You're now going to insert three lights. One to act as the sun, and the two of them to act as interior lights for the main building.

Time for action – creating Sunlight in Unity

1. Go to **GameObject ¦ Create Other ¦ Directional Light**.

2. Click on **Color** and select the shade you want. Slightly off-white is good. Then click on **x**.

3. With the light selected, click on the **Rotate** button as shown in the following screenshot. Now, use the cursor on the globe to rotate the light so that the rays are pointing tards the terrain.

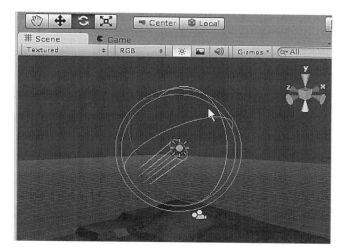

4. Now, select all the parameters in the **Inspector** panel in the next screenshot:

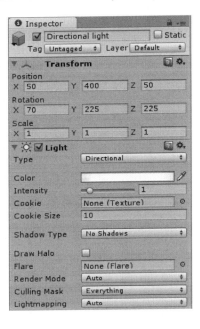

5. This is just an approximation of some daylight. I've placed the light high up, slightly to the left-hand side, and behind. Remember, x=0, y=0 is the bottom left-hand side of the map because that's where the **origin** was in SketchUp.

6. Label it **Daylight** in the box at the top, and press *Enter*.

7. Now, create another light in the same way—this time select the **Pointlight** option. Before you alter anything, click on the **Move** icon at the top of the screen. Use the Red, Blue, and Green arrows on the light to move it over the area in the center of where the industrial building will go.

8. Rotate your view with the middle and right-hand side mouse button so you can see the correct height too (See the next image):

9. When you're done, alter your **color**, **range,** and **intensity** to suit your preference. You can always come back and change this later.

10. If you wish, you can switch off the sunlight by clicking on it and un-checking the box in the **Inspector** pallet that says **Light**. This will let you see the strength of your second light more easily.

11. Label your new light **Indoor01**.

12. Now, right-click on it in the hierarchy, and select **Duplicate**.

13. Move this new light to the side a little, then label it—you guessed it!—**Indoor02**.

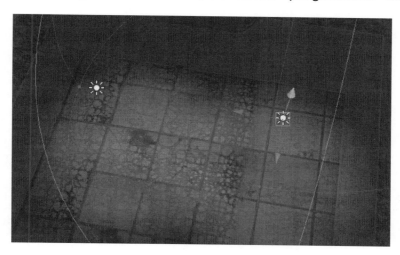

14. Turn your sunlight back on.

What just happened?

You set up one directional light to simulate sunlight, and two Omni lights to act as indoor lamps. The directional light is set high up (large Y-axis number) to simulate the sun. Because it's a directional light you had to adjust its tilt and rotation so that it's shown on the terrain. We placed it at an offset to one side so that you would get the effect of depth on the shaded portions of the terrain. The other two lights needed a number for range so that their effect wasn't too strong. You can see the range by the yellow globe around the light in the main view. Unfortunately, Unity free doesn't allow for realistic shadows from its lights; you need to pay for the Pro version for that.

Setting up your character controller

Unity 3D comes with two pre-packaged character controllers. All you need to do is grab them from the library and drag them in. The one we're using is called a **1st Person Controller** which allows you to see the level through the player character's eyes. Alternatively, you can select the **3rd Person Controller** which will let you see a little man walking around. These are the main two types of game controllers used with Unity 3D.

Time for action – setting up a first-person shooter style controller

1. In the **Project** tab, click on the arrow next to **Standard Assets,** and then select **Character Controllers**.

2. Click on **1st Person Controler** and drag it in to the main window.

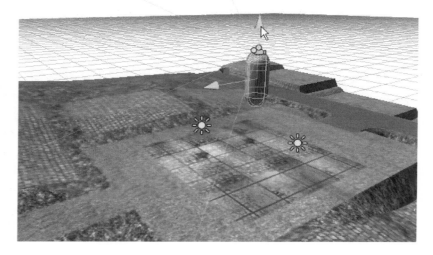

3. You will see the character depicted by a capsule-shaped object. You can move this around by dragging the arrows.

4. In **Transform** tab, under **Position**, type in **0,0,0** in the **x,y,z** fields, respectively.

5. Now, move the capsule around until it's over the starting point in the level. Notice when the capsule moves below the terrain it turns wire-framed. This is how you can work out how high or low to place it.

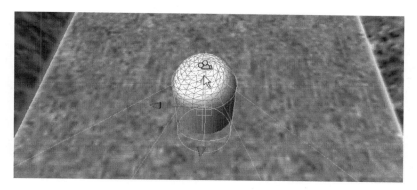

6. Place it so that the bottom is just above the floor.

7. Under **Transform** type **180** in the **Y Rotation** field. This faces your character along the path.

8. This character already has a camera attached to it, so, go ahead and delete the other one listed in the **Hierarchy** pallet. You don't need it.

9. Now go to **File ¦ Save Scene**.

What just happened?

You just set up your character controller and are ready to start walking around your level. Aren't you excited? The capsule you saw will not be there in the actual game. It's just a visual representation of your character, so that you can visualize where you're placing it, how big it is, and which direction it will face. You can change these things either by trial and error, or by inputting exact figures in the **Inspector**.

Time for action – playing the level

1. Click on the **Game** tab at the top of the screen.

2. At the top of your screen are a play, pause, and fast forward button. Press the **Play** button now!

3. Walk around using the arrow keys, and move your head using the mouse. Check that out for instant gratification!

Fall through the floor

If the only jaw that dropped was that of your game character falling through the floor, then go back to your character controller (the capsule thing) and move it up higher above the terrain. Now also check you've checked the generate colliders box in the **FBXImporter** tab when you select the terrain, as described earlier. Colliders describe which geometry is solid so that your character doesn't move through it.

4. Use the *Spacebar* to jump, too. You should have a first person view like the one above.

5. When you're done looking around your magnificent creation, click on the **Play** button again to return to the editor.

6. Wowsers! Was it really that simple? Yep. Now, check the following.

Time for action – creating a web playable walkthrough

1. Go to **File ¦ Build and Run**. Now, select **Web Player** and click on **Add Current** (see the next screenshot):

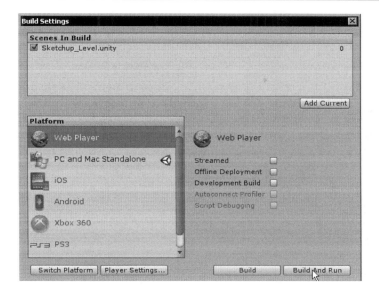

2. Click on **Build & Run**

3. Click on **Make New Folder** and add a folder with a random name to your desktop.

4. Click on **OK** and wait for the game to compile.

5. When a web page comes up, click **Install Now!**

6. On the Unity website click on **Install Now**. Run the file and follow the instructions.

7. Now go to your desktop and open the folder you created. Double-click on the `WebPlayer.htm` document.

8. Away you go in a web browser!

What just happened?

Unity is Middleware, which means it's a middle of the pipeline software program. It takes your assets, turns them into a game, and delivers them on as many gaming platforms as possible. You've just tried out one of them – Web. You can also deliver games to:

- PC
- Mac OS
- iOS (Apple's iPad, iPhone and iPod)

- Android (Google's mobile platform)
- Xbox 360
- PS3
- Wii

With the free version of Unity, you can publish to PC, Mac, and Web.

You can now see how easily a 3D environment is created and published with the SketchUp / Unity combo. You now have the skills to create a real-time walkthrough simulation of almost any environment. If you continue to study Unity, you can add to this foundation to any other gaming features you can think of.

 Packt Publishing has plenty of excellent Unity books to keep you going. You can find them all at http://www.packtpub.com/books/unity.

The character prefab you inserted into your game is a combination of code and objects that the creators of Unity have seen fit to give you along with the software. It's their way of showing you what can be done with the program. This is great for you and me, because it means that we can create a level and walk around it without any coding knowledge.

Pop quiz

a. What are the two main types of character controller included in Unity 3D?

b. What does the yellow globe around lights signify?

c. Which key should you press to center on your currently selected object?

d. How do you add collision detection to your terrain? What will happen if you don't?

Have a go hero

You know that fantastically realistic pallet you made in *Chapter 3, Wooden Pallet: Texture Creation*, and *Chapter 4, Wooden Pallet: Modeling*. How about inserting it into Unity? You've now developed the skills to do this. Follow the method in this chapter and insert the pallet this time instead of the terrain. It's just the same. Place it inside or to the side of the main building. Use the filename Pallet_gameready.

 If you haven't created the pallet yet you can use the file included in the download pack, labeled Chapter3_pallet_gameready.skp or you can use the exported file Pallet_Single.fbx and folder Pallet_Single, which I've also provided, placing them into the Sketchup4Games folder.

Here's what you should have when you're done:

Time for action – copying and pasting the pallet multiple times

Now it's time to stack some pallets one on top of one another. When you have a good asset, you might as well use it to full effect, don't you think?

1. In Unity, select the **Pallet_Single** object in the **Hierarchy** list. Go to **Edit ¦ Duplicate**.

2. Click on the **Move** icon and move the new pallet up using the green arrow.

3. Click on the **Rotate** icon and click on the **Pivot** button so that it changes to **Center**.

4. Use the green part of the sphere outline to rotate the copy of the pallet.

5. Select both pallets in the hierarchy list. Hold down *Ctrl* (*Cmd* on the Mac) to select multiple objects.

6. Now repeat steps 2-4.

7. Repeat again depending on how big you want the stack to be!

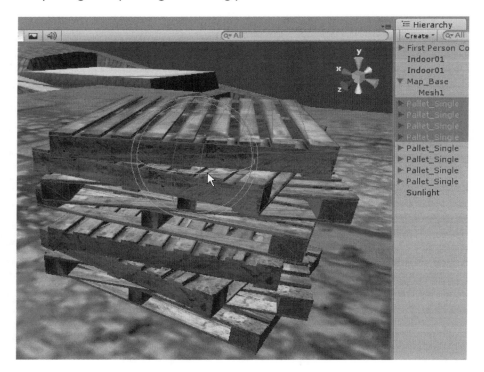

8. Now, to get one pallet leaning against the others, **Duplicate** a single pallet as done before.

9. Move it out to the side of the others.

10. Use the blue part of the rotate sphere to turn it on its side.

11. Use **Move tool** to move it against the other pallets.

12. Now you've got a stack of them. No point in wasting a good asset! Save your scene and project, and click on **Play** to see what it looks like in the game.

What just happened?

As you can see, Unity has its own Move, Copy, and Rotate functions different to those you used in SketchUp, but they do the same thing. It's worth spending some time using these features of Unity so that you get used to them. It will save you having to re-export from SketchUp each time you make a change.

Summary

Yes, you've gone and done it now. Game design addiction awaits. In this chapter, you figured out how to:

- Export from SketchUp and Import into **Unity 3D**, a full featured professional **game development environment**.
- Reattach your high resolution texture.
- Scale and move objects in Unity.
- Find your way around the Unity interface.
- Create lights: sunshine and indoor.
- Control light parameters: Range, Color and Intensity.
- Duplicate and manipulate assets.
- Publish your game to the Web.
- Walk (and jump) around your terrain!

If I were you, I would now take a deep breath, put my coat on and go for a walk. You need some time to think about what you're going to do with this amazing new skill set. I'm not just exaggerating here. The ability to easily publish 3D environments anywhere, to be used by anyone, and to explore them in real time, is only just now becoming a mainstream reality. You're now at the forefront of it. Make the most of that.

When you get back it's time to get down to some hard work. Playtime's over, and it's high time you filled your level with some realistic assets. In the next chapters, you will learn how to create standard assets such as buildings, trees, vehicles... and rusty dilapidated fencing.

7
Quick Standard Assets

You're a student. One day you wake up and your room looks different. You can't quite put your finger on why. It just looks wrong, somehow, well... bigger. You roll over and slap your face on the bare floorboards. Instantly you're awake. You understand. Your bed's gone. So is your pillow, sheets, the wardrobe, your chair, and the bedside cabinet. In fact, it's all gone. You leap up and bound down the stairs to face your housemates. They've left you a note on the kitchen table: "You can have your stuff back, as long as you can remember what was there. Whatever you can't remember goes to the dumpster." You think, "Where did I get such hilarious housemates?" but you're uneasy. What did I have in my room?

We all get so used to stuff that we don't really see it anymore. That is, unless you're one of those people with a photographic memory. Most of us aren't. Take it all away and we won't be able to tell what we're missing—just that things don't look right. Rooms and places are sterile without random things and junk. A little empty, but we don't know why. That's worth bearing in mind as a game artist. Most of your job is down to seducing the player into thinking they're in a real place. If the place feels sterile, empty, you've failed. The answer to this is to start paying attention to the world you live in - and that starts with the room, bus, train carriage, or plane you're in now.

Ask yourself—is this place neatly organized? Is this stuff where it's supposed to be, orderly, or just lying around? Is that table straight or at an angle with the wall? Is the sheet on that bed ironed or crumpled? Is that bag or suitcase new and shiny or a little bit worse to wear? Have the objects that are here perhaps seen better days?

As an asset and level creator it's actually best to lean on the side of worn, weary and aged than neat, orderly and new. That's what we'll base this chapter on. Let's create some standard assets that are going to give a sense of life to the scene, without stealing the show. You should almost not notice them, but if someone took them away, you'd feel something was wrong.

In this chapter you will learn how to:

- Build a fence with posts and wire mesh
- Quickly generate believable buildings
- Import and clean up 3D-Warehouse models for game use
- Generate quick standard assets such as barrels and tools

Along the way you'll pick up loads more SketchUp skills. You'll also practice what you already know from the previous chapters.

Rough and ready fencing

There's nothing better than some fencing when you want to keep the player out of areas you've not had time to fill with assets. There's a fringe benefit, too. The more you keep them away, the more they will try to get in, which keeps them playing. Fencing also looks good, but only when you follow my one-step plan:

- Make it as grubby as you can

Yes, make it as grubby, shabby, and broken down as is allowable within your overall game style. There's nothing more appealing in games than old broken stuff. Having old, broken, messy stuff lying around everywhere makes us feel like we're really living in the game. I used to really live when I was a student.

Time for action – making fencing with SketchUp's materials

We've not yet used the materials much that came bundled with SketchUp. If you haven't downloaded the full extended set yet, head over to *Chapter 2, Tools that Grow on Trees* now and find out how.

1. In SketchUp open up a default template with a 2D person present to help you with scale. Select the meters template.

2. Draw a rectangle and type **0.2,0.2** and hit *Enter*.

3. **Push/Pull** to a little over the height of the person.

4. Now, make it into a component and copy it for a distance of 2m.

5. Draw a rectangle from the bottom of one pillar to almost the top of the next pillar, as you can see in the next screenshot:

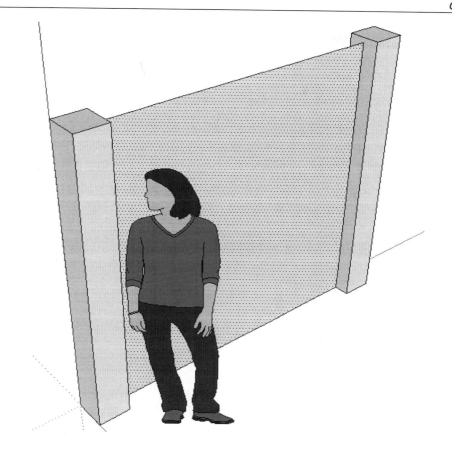

6.   Now, select the **Paint Bucket** tool and select **Fencing** in the **Materials** pallet.

7.   Select one of the wire mesh materials and paint it onto the rectangle on both sides.

8.   Go to CGTextures.com and select **Metal ¦ Painted** and select any of the textures you like—one that you can get a reasonable area of metal from.

9.   Prepare the texture as you've done before in *Chapter 3, Wooden Pallet*: *Texture Creation* and *Chapter 5, Game Levels in SketchUp*, or just import it straight into SketchUp.

10. Double-click to edit one of the posts and apply it to each of the four sides of the post, as you learned in *Chapter 4, Wooden Pallet: Modeling*, using **Import** and **Use as Texture**.

11. Alter the position and rotation if you need to for each face.

12. Copy the edges of one face as shown next so that they are offset by 0.02

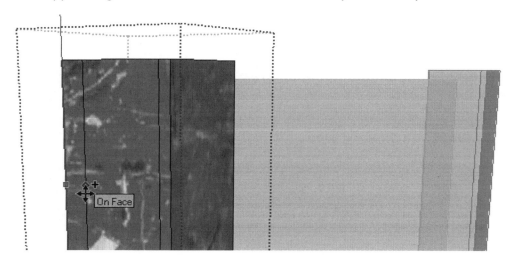

13. Do the same for the opposite side. Now **Push/Pull** to indent each of these new faces as you can see in the next screenshot.

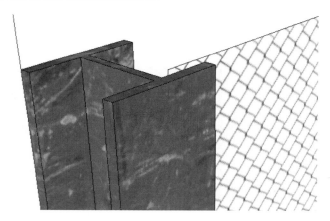

14. Move the left edge of the fence panel to touch the inside of the post, then repeat with the right edge.

What just happened?

The mesh material that you applied to the fence panel is see-through, apart from the mesh wire. This is because the PNG image used in the texture has an alpha channel. This tells SketchUp what to display, and what to leave see through. Now, it's time to save your fence and make it ready for duplication all over your level.

Time for action – making several unique variations

1. Delete the second post.

2. Save the SketchUp file as `FencePanelMASTER.skp`.

3. Go to **File ¦ Save As** and save it again as `FencePanelV01.skp`. This is going to be your first variant.

4. Select some of the textures in the column and move them around a little, rescale or skew them as you learned in *Chapter 4, Wooden Pallet: Modeling*.

5. Save the file and close it.

6. Open the master version and save as `FencePanelV02.skp`.

7. Right-click on the fence panel and select **Make Unique Texture**.

8. Now, right-click again and select **Texture ¦ Edit Texture Image**

9. Your fence panel will open in GIMP.

10. Use the **Eraser Tool** to make some jagged holes.

11. Add a poster, sign, or pieces of paper from the **Posters** and **Stickers** category on `CGTextures.com` as a new layer

12. Go to **Layer ¦ Scale Layer** if you need to make it smaller.

13. Use the **Layer Masks** feature, or **Eraser Tool** in GIMP to get rid of the bits you don't need as you can see next:

14. When you're done vandalizing your fence, go to **Layer ¦ Merge Down**.

15. Go to **File ¦ Save**. Then close the GIMP window with the **x** at the top right.

16. SketchUp updates with the new image:

What just happened?

SketchUp allows you to make a unique image based on a face in the model. When you edit it, it retains the properties of the base texture that you applied to it. So, in this case, the image had the see-through bits (**Alpha channel**) applied correctly. When you added another image over the top, masked bits out, and then merged the layers together, that see-through alpha channel remained intact.

You've now got three different variations of the same fence. Go ahead and make some more!

Have a go hero – deforming stuff for added realism

Imagine that this fence has been there for donkey's years. What would it really look like? Would it be a flat panel if it had been climbed and jumped over a thousand times by neighborhood kids? Of course not! How are you going to make the panel saggy at the top? Actually, you already learned how to do this in *Chapter 5, 3D games in SketchUp*, when you covered the sandbox tools. If you're feeling adventurous now, give it a go!

Create the panel flat to the ground and rotate it into place when you're done. Or even better, leave one version where it is and use a component copied and rotated at 90 degrees to work on with the sandbox tools.

Alternatively, if you're becoming a dab hand at GIMP or PhotoShop, edit the texture inside to simulate the sagging mesh fence. You can try the **Smudge** tool or experiment with many other deform tools.

Inserting multiple copies to quickly fill out a level

It's now time to create the entire fenced area of your level in SketchUp. You can then import it to Unity. You learned how to do that in *Chapter 6, Importing to a Professional Game Application*: *Unity 3D*, so we won't cover it again here. Doing the repetitive work of copying and manipulating multiple versions within SketchUp is much quicker than doing it in a game engine. This is especially true when you are trying to quickly scope out a level to see if it works visually and spatially.

 Instances
Copying the asset around in the game engine, however, is likely to give you speed gains within the game, as engines are designed to handle copies as **instances**. This is where an asset is loaded into the memory of the computer just once, even though you can see it multiple times.

The workflow for copying around any large number of objects is similar to the following. This method will allow you to fill your level with stuff very quickly:

1. Import the master object into the SketchUp level
2. Copy it wherever you need it
3. Select a few and make them unique
4. Swap them for another version
5. Repeat the last two steps with further versions
6. Create further variation by scaling or mirroring some objects

Time for action – fencing large areas

1. Open up your level master in SketchUp. Yours will be called
   `Map_Base_Master.skp` or you can use the one from the download
   pack named `Chapter5_Terrain_Textured.skp`.

2. Import the first version of your asset. This should be the one called
   `FencePanelMASTER.skp`.

3. Move it into position as shown next:

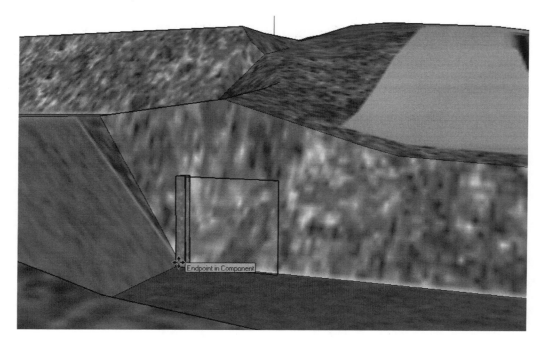

4. Now to copy it several times along the path, remember that we set the posts at
   2m apart. If you now copy the fence using the **Move** tool and holding *Ctrl* (*Option*
   on the Mac) along the Green Axis, then type **2** and *Enter*, you should get the panel
   lined up correctly.

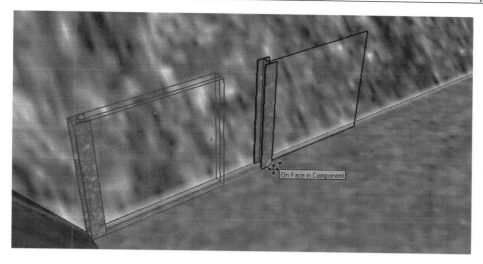

5. Now type **10x** and *Enter*. You should get ten versions of the fence, all spaced at 2m intervals!

6. Copy the end fence so that the post is at the corner of the concrete yard. Now, use the **Rotate** tool to rotate on a right angle.

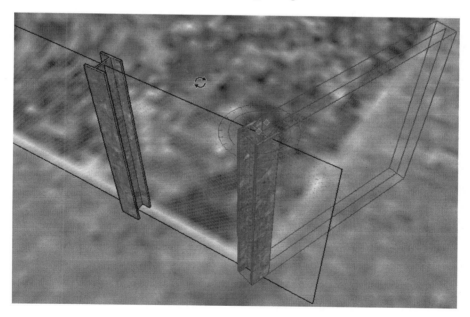

7. Right-click on the end panel and click on **Make Unique**. Now, shorten the fence panel so that the edge just touches the column.

8. Carry on with these steps until you've done one side of the yard as shown here:

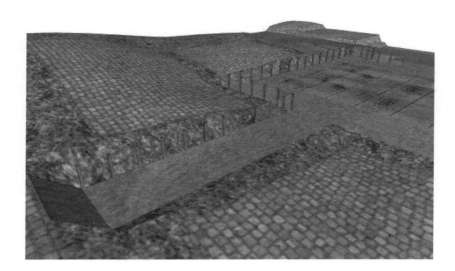

9. Open the **Outliner** pallet. Select all of the fences.

Tip for quick selection by name

Type **fence** into the box at the top of the outliner. It will now show only the items within your model that have **fence** in their names.

10. Now right-click and select **Make Group** as shown next:

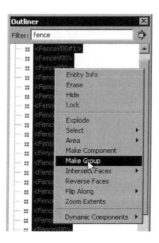

11. Copy the group. Right-click on it and select **Flip Along ¦ Group's Red**.

12. Move the new group into place. You should now have fencing all round the concrete yard and path.

13. Open the group and move or copy any fence panels that don't fit. You're done!

What just happened?

With minimum effort, you covered a large area of your level with interesting assets. This was possible because you made a few variations of a simple asset, and then re-used it multiple times. The asset was set up to work with a 2m grid which further speeds up placement. Finally, SketchUp's great tool set allowed you to do this job probably far quicker and more easily than other 3D tools.

You can use this technique in your future career to great effect whenever you're up against a tough deadline. Using the same thing over and over again allows you to quickly see what your level will look like so you can make changes to the scope of the level without having to go back to the drawing board. SketchUp is a great preliminary visualization tool.

Time for action – walking around in SketchUp to visualize your level

1. Go to **Camera ¦ Walk**.

2. Type in **1.8** and hit enter.

3. Hold the left-hand side mouse button and drag the mouse up or down to walk forward or backwards.

4. Now, use your right-click menu to select **Look Around**

5. Walk around using a combination of **Walk** and **Look Around** to see how your level will look in a first person game.

Have a go hero – swapping in your variations

You're now ready for *Step 3* in this method. Explode the fencing groups first. Select some fences at random. Make them unique. Now, select one of these new components, right-click and select Reload. Select a new component (V01, V02, and so on). Repeat it with your other variants.

Use the following techniques to further mess it up:

- Move a number of fences in and out, so they're not all exactly in line
- Flip a few by the red axis to create a mirror copy
- Scale a few in the blue axis to make them slightly shorter
- Use the **Rotate** tool to lean the posts in or out
- Use the **Rotate** tool to rotate components in plan
- Think of creative ways to add a sense of realism on your own!

You can use the `Chapter7_Map_Base_with_fence.skp` file to experiment on.

Generating buildings quickly

When generating buildings, think modular! All the good game designers do this. They decide on a visual theme for the current level, and then generate a few building components that fit together well and that can be placed throughout the level. These buildings are fillers. You will learn how to create a more detailed building (which can also be explored inside) in *Chapter 9, The Main Building — Inside and Out*. For now, the name of the game is speed.

 For this quick method, you will need to find and download some building frontage textures from somewhere like CGTextures.com. Go for full buildings and some generic images, such as the side or rear of a disused building. Also, grab a couple of windows and shutter doors.

Time for action – creating a building from two images

1. Start with a rectangle roughly the size of your building and **Push/Pull** it into a box.

2. Import the front of a building and select **Use as Texture**.

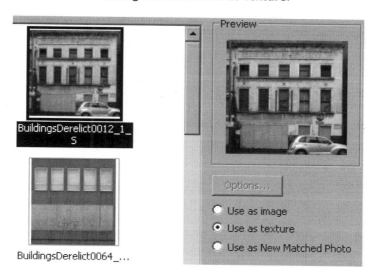

3. Place it on the bottom left corner of the front face of your box and click to the top right as shown next.

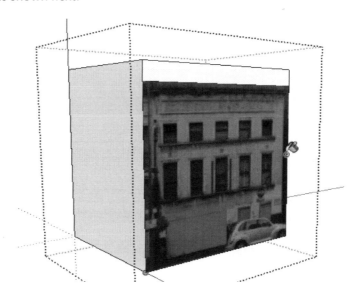

4. Now, **Push/Pull** the sides and roof of the box so that the edges line up nicely with the edge of the building in the image.

5. Add a generic image on the side in the same way. Here's the model so far:

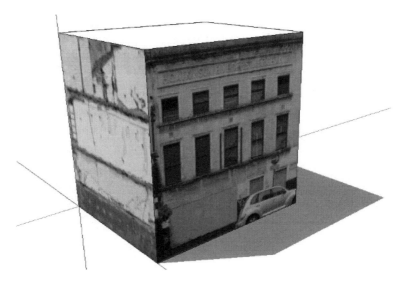

6. Use a normal SketchUp material on the roof.

7. Double-click the roof to select the sides of the roof, then use the offset tool to create a narrow frame around the edge. Push/pull the inner rectangle down a little to create a parapet and flat roof. Your game characters will be able to walk on this.

8. Right-click on the front image and select **Texture ¦ Make Unique Texture**. Now select **Texture** again and select **Edit Texture** Image. This will take you to GIMP.

9. In GIMP, paste the image of a shutter door or whatever else you like onto the base texture.

10. When you're done, flatten the image and save it. Exit GIMP.

11. The image will update in SketchUp. Sample and paint the new texture onto the back wall too, and do the same with the left side onto the right side face.

12. Here's my completed building:

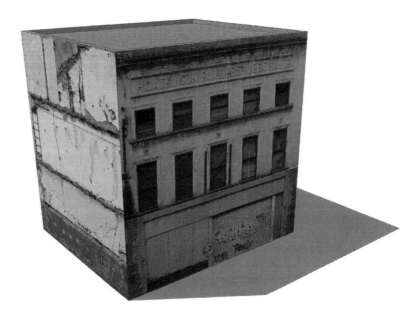

Have a go hero – modular generic building elements

Try one or two generic-looking building faces and make modular building blocks out of them. Here's one made from an ugly-looking building façade of an office:

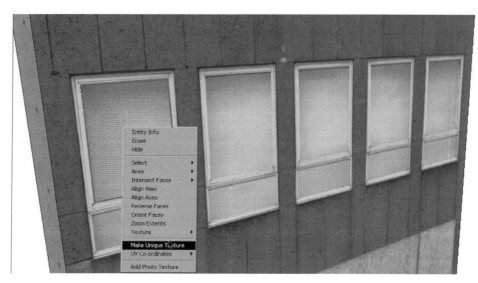

Create a rectangle of one of the windows and make it unique as you can see in the previous screenshot. Now, you will be able to copy that window to the other windows. This is so that you have the option of making this material reflective in your game engine later.

Once you've made a modular building façade, try copying it multiple times using the **Move** tool (explained in *Chapter 4, Wooden Pallet: Modeling*) to see what you get:

I rendered this one with the free version of Shaderlight to see if the reflective windows worked okay. It's not a bad result for about 30 minutes modeling and rendering.

When the going gets tough

When the drill sergeant shouts out, "There's a dangerous secret mission behind the enemy lines and I need volunteers! I need 'em now! This will be dangerous. Most of you will not come back alive. So, don't be shy! Who's with me?" and you, naturally, take a step backwards. But when you look around you to see who has volunteered... you notice there's only you in the parade ground.

The thing is, it's all very well being a one-man (or woman) team. It's all quite rosy being a one-man army, a single-boy band, a Unity, in fact. That is until things take a turn for the worst and you find yourself up a river without a paddle. You're bored of slaving away at your computer in isolation, you're stuck for ideas, stuck for time, and just plain stuck.

Many people involved in games hit this wall. It happens when you start your game project thinking, "This is going to be Great! This is going to be amazing! And, I'll do it all by myself!" You see this kind of thing on the forums all the time:

> *"I'm doing a first person shooter in the style of [some big title]. Here's my progress so far! What do you guys think of THIS!!?"*

Then, there follows a couple of small images. The first of a gun (un-textured). The second of maybe a crate (sometimes textured). The third (if there is a third) of another gun (un-textured and a bit like the first one). The forum replies come through thick and fast, and they're not very complimentary.

This particular kind of mania is actually quite normal for us compulsive gaming types. No one told us that creating a FPS in the style of *Rambo goes to Mars in a Taxi* (by Epic Games) was this much work, so we're not really to blame. The fact that the list of credits at the end of any commercially released game takes longer to scroll through than it took to complete the game itself is lost on us... because we're a one man army! We've volunteered our multiple self for the mission and we're going to finish it until it kills us!

I'd like to give you a few forum posts as examples of those asset creators who have started off well but crashed and burned—there are so many to choose from—but that would be cruel. Although we can't throw stones; we're all just as susceptible. This chapter is there for all of us when we hit the wall. We realize we overestimated our abilities, time, and dedication, and we're prepared to admit it. So, what do we do now? Well, that's easy. We do what we always do in situations like this.

We cheat, of course!

Using someone else's assets

Now I know that your dad told you cheating was wrong, but hey! We all know there are different kinds of cheating. There's the wrong kind and then there's the kind of cheating that's not really cheating at all. The thing is, if people leave their stuff lying around on the Internet for all to see and download, why would it be so wrong to stick some of it in your game? Actually, it can be very necessary. If you don't do it, often your game level won't get finished, and then no one gets to see how great your skills are. Assets taken from the Internet can provide much needed "context" to your own modeling. Just make sure you don't claim to have created anything that was actually created by others.

Assets that you find on the Internet were once created by somebody, and that person owns the copyright. Don't ever stick assets into a game if you don't know where they came from and have permission to use them. When creating a sample game for your portfolio, or testing a game level with some sample assets, using what you find on the Internet is unlikely to be a problem.

Everyone in the game industry has a specific job. In big games, their job might be just to do lighting all day. That's all they do for the whole game. They also might model terrain assets and nothing else. Even the texturing will be done by a colleague. Here we have a quandary. If you are to realistically test out your skills as a game artist in a close-to-real life environment, it will only happen if you are part of a team. There's no way someone would let you loose on a whole level like I'm doing in this book. To be honest, it's just too much work for one person. The skill you really need to learn next is how to make use of someone else's assets. It just so happens that it'll also noticeably speed up your own job! Everyone's a winner when we cheat (in a good way).

Time for action – cleaning up a Google Warehouse model

Let's go and get a building from the 3D Warehouse and get it up to scratch so that it's worthy of being included in our level.

1. Navigate to `sketchup.google.com/3dwarehouse/`.

2. Type in your search for the type of building you want.

3. Download the model and open it in SketchUp. Here is one I found:

4. Looks terrific, but before we import it into our game engine, it is best to check a few things:

- ° Correct Scale
- ° If there are too many groups or components
- ° Textures applied sensibly
- ° All faces orientated outwards
- ° At origin
- ° At right angles to Green and Red axes

Fixing the origin and removing hidden geometry

1. First things first, what about the origin point? The building needs to be at the origin, and lined up with the Green and Red axes so that when you insert the component in your level it will insert where you want it first time.

2. There could also be a lot of hidden things in the model, too. The easiest way to deal with these issues is to copy and paste the model into a new file.

3. Select the building, right click and select **Explode**.

4. Select the whole building again and go to **Edit ¦ Copy**

5. Now go to **File ¦ New**.

6. Paste the building in this new file (**Edit ¦ Paste**).

7. Now hit **M** for **Move** and click the corner of the building.

8. Move it to the origin point and click to drop it there.

9. Use the **Rotate** tool and click at the origin making sure it goes blue first. This means the rotate action will happen around the blue axis.

10. Now, click somewhere along the front straight edge of the building as shown next:

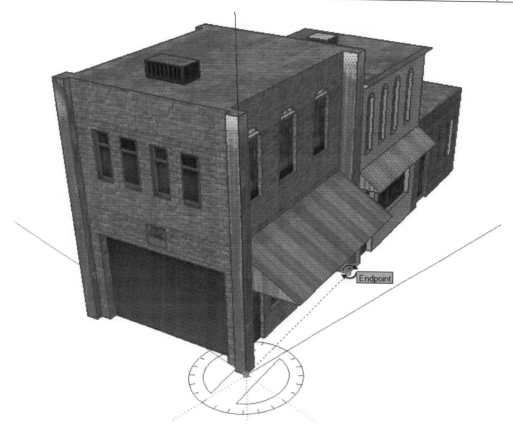

11. Move it on to the Red axis until it snaps there and click. You now have the building lined up with the Red and Green axes.

Rectifying scale issues

1. Now, let's check the scale:

2. First, we'll set the units within SketchUp to Meters. Do this in **Window ¦ Model Info ¦ Units**.

3. Use the **Tape Measure** tool to measure the height of a doorway. This is a pretty foolproof way of scaling a building. It should always be around 2m, so type in **2** then *Enter*. Click **Yes** to re-scale the model.

4. You now have a scaled model in the right place, and have removed most of the extra bits and pieces someone might have accidentally left in the file.

Checking face alignment and textures

1. All faces in SketchUp have a back and front. It is very important in gaming for faces to be the right way round. Click on the **Monochrome view** button.

2. You should only see white faces. If you see any blue ones, right click and select **Reverse Faces**.

3. Hang on - there's still textures showing in this model. That's because there's some groups or components that haven't been exploded yet. Select everything again and **Explode**.

4. When you have only white faces showing, click the **Shaded with Textures** button again.

5. You might notice if you have reversed any faces the texture will have disappeared. Select these faces one face at a time and re-apply the texture that was there before.

6. You might need to use the sample tool in the materials pallet to copy textures from one window to another as shown here. Then use **right click ¦ Texture ¦ Position** to move them into place.

What just happened?

You imported a model from the 3D Warehouse and did some work on it to bring it up to the standard needed in your game. You can use this method on anything you download and import, not just from the 3D Warehouse. It is not advised to import straight into your game because game engines are very picky about textures and reversed faces. If the back side of a face is showing it will look fine in SketchUp, but in the game it will be entirely see-through.

The ten-minute oil barrel

No level is complete without more rusty, ugly, junk. This one's really quick and that's why you'll find it in most games. The word for it is "ubiquitous." Rather a posh word to use for a battered barrel.

1. Import the image into a new SketchUp project using the **As Image** setting.

2. Scale the image so that it's about one meter tall. Move it so that the center passes though the Blue axis as shown here.

3. Move the image down a little so that no part of the base of the barrel is above the Green axis, as you can see in the previous screenshot.

4. Now click the **Circle** tool and type in **8** then *Enter*. This sets the number of segments to **8**.

5. Place the cursor on the Red or Green axis. Hold *Shift* to lock it to that axis, and click on the origin point.

6. Now, click somewhere near the edge of the barrel, but not quite the edge, as shown next:

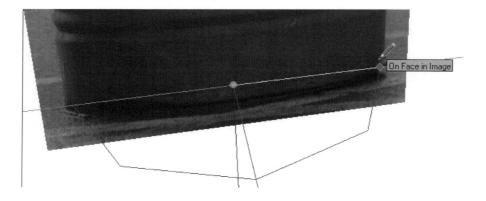

7. A circle appears. Use the **Push/Pull** tool to pull the face to nearly the top of the barrel.

8. Now, select the image and **Move** it away from the cylinder. Right-click on it and **Explode**.

9. Get the **Sample Paint** tool from the **Materials pallet** and click on the image. Now paint the cylinder and the barrel texture appears!

10. Use an untidy steel material for the top of the barrel or find a texture on the Internet showing the top of a barrel if you want added realism.

11. That's it! A low-polygon asset! I know it looks blocky, but that also means it has a low polygon count, with a low file size. You can now use this all over your game level without slowing game play down.

Creating tools or weapons

The character we're going to insert in our level is of a car mechanic. He needs some extra tools. We're going to make a simple 3D wrench in this tutorial, but the principles can be carried through to any tool, prop, or weapon you'd like to make. Essentially, we're going to trace the outline of the texture image and then raise or lower parts of it.

Time for action – modeling a low polygon wrench

1. First, find an image with a side on view of your wrench. Here's mine:

2. Import it into SketchUp. Set the plan view and go to **Camera ¦ Parallel Projection**.

3. Take out your pencil and draw around the outline. Remember this is going to have to be low polygon, so use as few clicks of the mouse as you can.

4. Start with the curves, because these look circular, and so you will be able to use the **Arc** tool. When you click the tool, type in **3** (or **4**) and *Enter*. All the arcs you draw will now have only 3 (or 4) sides to them, as shown next:

5. When you've drawn in the curves, finish the outline off with the pencil tool.

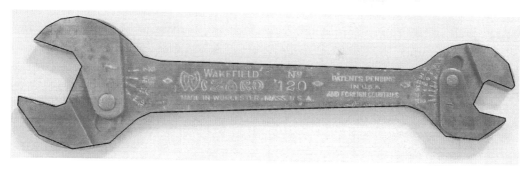

6. You can now **Push/Pull** the wrench out to give it some dimension.

7. Move the image away from the wrench using the **Move** tool. Now, explode the image.

8. Use the **Sample Paint** tool in the **Materials** pallet to sample the image, then paint it onto the top face of the wrench. Now it looks like we're getting somewhere!

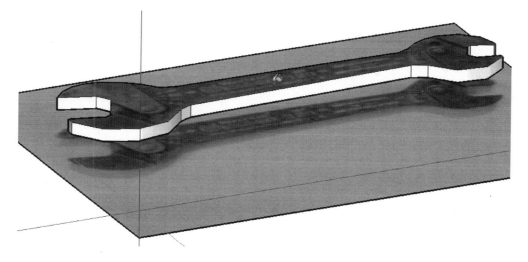

9. Use the pencil or arc tools to trace over the internal parts that you wish to push in or pull out. Keep it all nice and simple as you can see here.

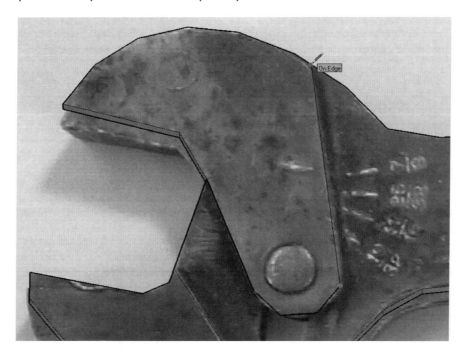

10. When you're done, use **Push/Pull** on the areas you've just created to raise or lower them.

11. Getting a balance between modeled detail, and detail that's best left to the texture comes with experience.

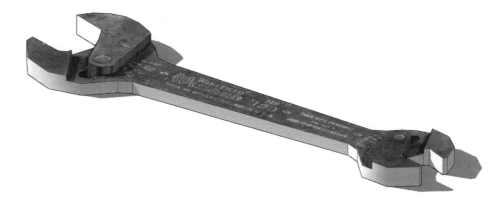

12. Now in GIMP, open your wrench image and use the **Smudge** tool to smudge the colour at the edges of the wrench outwards as much as you can, like so.

13. Save the image with a new name. Now here comes the trick. This trick allows you to model most 3D objects without any more than a single photo view of the object.

14. In SketchUp go to the Materials pallet. Select your photo of the wrench and go to the edit tab. Click Browse, and load in the blurred version of the image.

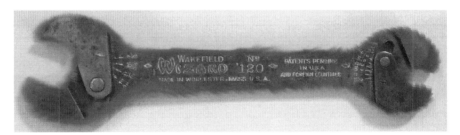

15. Select just the bottom face of your wrench. Now use the **Scale** tool and carefully expand it slightly in one direction, using the *Ctrl* key (*Cmd* on the Mac) to scale about the center, as you can see here.

16. Triple-click to select the whole model. Now use the **Sample Paint** tool in the **Materials pallet** again to sample the image, then paint it onto the model.

17. The bevelled edge you created now takes on the colour that you blurred outwards in GIMP.

18. Delete the image and delete the bottom face of the wrench.

19. Select the whole wrench and turn it into a **Group**. Copy it down the Blue axis, and then use **Flip Along ⁞ Group's Blue Axis**.

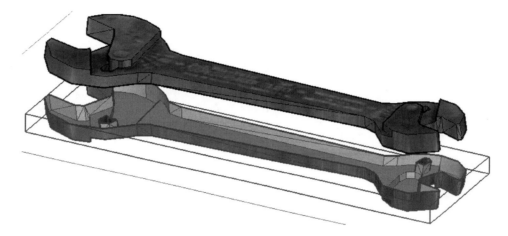

20. You now have two sides of the wrench. **Explode** them both and use **Move** along the Blue axis to join them together.

The previous image is a quick render in Shaderlight, a free rendering plugin, and the SketchUp version shown next.

What just happened?

You've created an asset using the simple but effective image modeling method that SketchUp is so good at. You did this by simply creating a 3D outline and then Push/Pulling parts of it until you got the shape you wanted. You also learned a trick to allow you to use a single plan image, without the side views, to texture your model. There are lots of props that can benefit from this method.

Summary

In this chapter, you have applied all your skills learned so far. You've stretched yourself a little more too. To sum up, you learned:

- How to save time and create variation in the scene by reusing multiple versions of the same asset repeatedly
- How to mess up the scene for added realism by scaling, moving, flipping, leaning, and otherwise vandalising your assets
- How to import, clean up, and modify existing assets for re-use
- Some specific asset modeling tricks to make common props
- Some quick modular-building creation methods

By now you should be experimenting by yourself and creating lots of other assets using the techniques you've learned so far. In the next two chapters, you will be taking these skills further to create progressively more complex assets. From now on, the pace will get a little faster, and you may need to flick back a few chapters every so often just to review something you learned earlier. You can now choose to go on and model the main building and some trees, or you can jump to the end of the book where you will load it all into Unity and set up your game simulation. Either way, congratulations are in order for graduating from the SketchUp school of Asset Design. First class!

Your graduation present is a rusty wrench.

8

Advanced Modeling: Create a Realistic Car in Easy Steps

I know what you've been going through. You've been busy for hours learning how to put a rusty fence together and carefully placing it all around your level. You then show it to your nearest and dearest and they say, "Um... that's nice dear," or "Why does it look so rusty? Should it be rusty?," and you go from feeling ecstatic at your achievement, to feeling like a loser in the space of a few minutes.

The reason you don't get the "Oohs" and "Aahs" right away is because people are used to seeing completed games—the ones that took the team of hundreds of people a few years to complete. Compare what you can do now with what you could do before, and you're safe in your own knowledge of what you have achieved. Always remember—all those games are made up of individual efforts, like yours, by individuals, like you.

There is, however, a place for showing off, and that place is here at the end of our book. Now that your skills are up to it, you're going to make something that people not "in the know" can be immediately impressed by. A posh car!

Where to find car images and plans

Because a majority of us don't have sculpting skills, our car is going to be made by applying logical steps and techniques. It will, therefore, only be as good as the plans and photos we base it on, and because I don't expect you to be a sculptor, we're going to cheat once more and use the image modeling techniques SketchUp is so good at. Only this time, we will add line drawings to our photo textures in combination.

Access `http://www.the-blueprints.com`. Sign up for a free account and have a good look around. See anything you like? Any of these cars can be yours when you learn the techniques in this chapter!

Time for action – creating a car texture

1. Use the search feature on `http://www.the-blueprints.com` to find the **Mercedes CL 2010** plans. If you need to you can enter this URL instead: http://www.the-blueprints.com/blueprints/cars/mercedes/42052/viewsingle/ mercedes-benz_cl-class_(2010)/.

2. Download the plan and open it in GIMP. You should see the following:

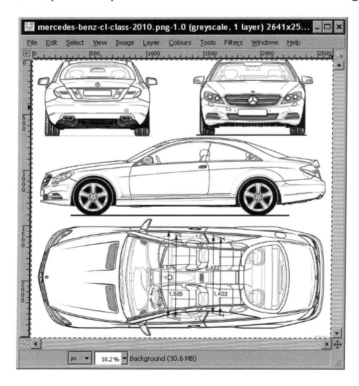

Notice how you have the whole car described here in four views? From top left-hand side to bottom: Back view, Front view, Left side view, Plan. We don't need any more views than this because the right-hand side is the same as the left-hand side, and the bottom of the car is immaterial. These views are called *Orthographic* views, and are commonly used in technical drawing. You will need Orthographic views to make cars because they aren't distorted like perspective or camera views.

3. If the image is not a square, use the crop tool to make it a square, and then resize the image to 4096x4096 or 2048x2048.

4. Perform a **Save As** to save your `.xcf` master file, and then use **Save a Copy** for a `.jpg` called `MB_ambient_2048.jpg`.

5. This second image is what you will be using in SketchUp.

6. Import the image into SketchUp using **File ¦ Import** and select **jpg image**, then check the **Use as Image** box.

7. Place the image in SketchUp. Use the **Tape Measure** tool to click at the end of one of the dimension lines, then click at the other end. Then type in the measurement and press **Enter**. Accept the resize action by clicking on **Yes**.

8. Your image is now correctly to scale. Right-click on it and click **explode**.

9. Divide it into four sections using the **Pencil** tool. Then make a group out of each section by double-clicking and selecting **Make Group** in the right click on the menu. You'll see it in the following screenshot:

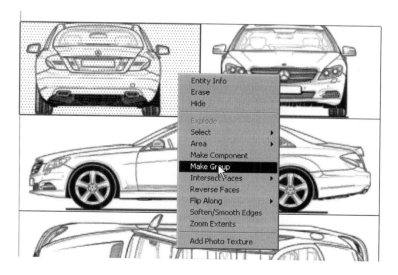

10. Once grouped, rotate each of the front, back, and side views upright.

11. Now move the side view, front view, and back view images so that the baseline lines up with the plan image as you can see following screenshot:

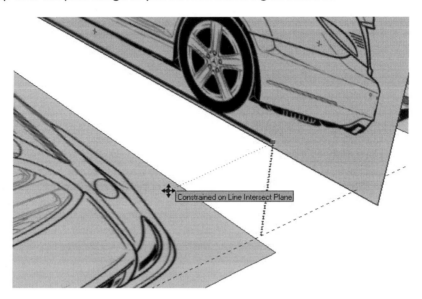

12. Use the **Tape Measure** tool to set a construction line at the farthest front and back point of the car on the Plan view, as you can see in the following screenshot. Do this by first clicking on the edge and moving the tape measure parallel to it.

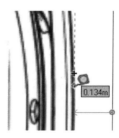

13. Draw further construction lines at the very center of the plan, front and rear images. Use the Mercedes Benz logo to line them up correctly.

14. Now divide each of these images in two parts with the **Pencil** tool by drawing along the construction lines. Delete the right-hand sides.

15. Move all the pieces in one place as you can see in the next image. Use the construction lines to line up the side image with the plan.

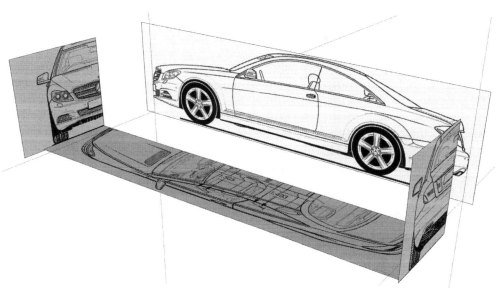

16. Now, using as few lines as possible, draw around each of the plans, both sides and one-end view. Just include the overall shape, and forget about the wing mirrors.

17. You now have outlines of each view. If you switch to **Monochrome** view, your outline is visible and should look something like the next image:

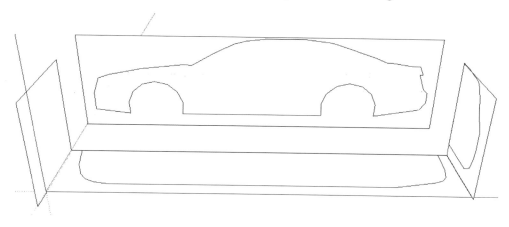

What just happened?

You've taken an orthographic car drawing and cut it into its individual views. Plan, Front, Rear, and Side views. You've placed them back where they came from in the first place. If you think about it, someone looked at a real car (which is a 3D object) from the front, rear, side, and from above, and drew what they saw. In order for you to recreate the 3D object, you need to arrange the 2D drawings to replicate where they were in the first place.

Now that you've drawn round the outside outline of the car from three directions, you can use these to create a 3D outline.

Time for action – creating a 3D car outline

1. Use **Push/Pull** on the side view to extrude the car's outline as far as the edge of the plan goes. You can see this here.

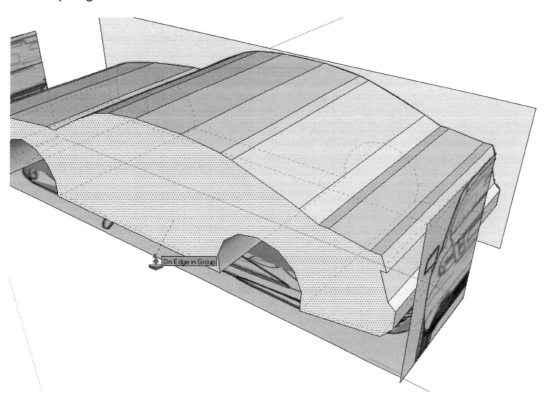

2. Now do the same with the rear view. Triple-click on it to select everything, and then right-click and select **Intersect Faces ¦ With Model**.

Boolean tools

If you have SketchUp Pro, skip to step 7. You can use SketchUp Pro's **Boolean tools** to do the following steps.

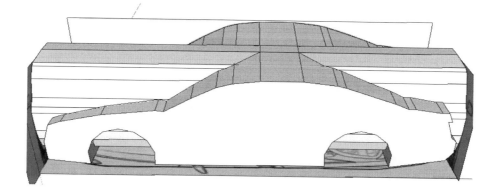

3. The part you want to keep is where the two volumes intersect. Use the eraser on everything that falls outside both outlines, as you can see here.

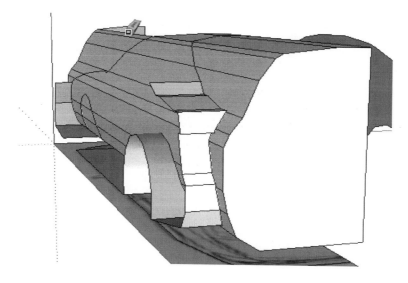

4. Once you've finished, you should already have the following basic car shape. You can now hide the images to see your model better.

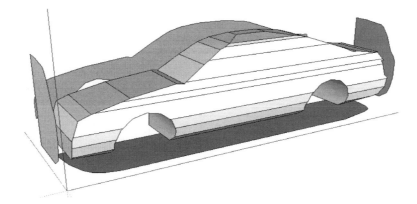

5. Now to finish off, extrude the plan shape and again use **Intersect with Model**.

6. Delete the parts you don't need.

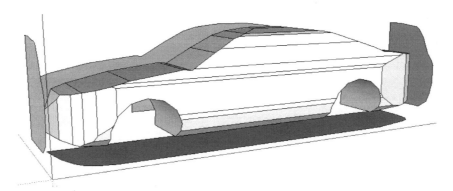

7. If you have SketchUp Pro you can do this much easier using the Solid Tools. Here's how. After extruding each part, turn it into a **Group**.

8. Select your three groups. Then simply go to **Tools ¦ Solid Tools ¦ Intersect**. You're done!

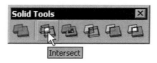

What just happened?

You've just created a car body using simple, foolproof steps. This rough form represents the basic 3D outline of half of your car. You will duplicate and flip it so that it creates a full car. The form you have in front of you is already good enough for a low-polygon game asset mesh. It just needs a realistic texture. When you think about how quickly you could apply this method to creating any car, you can see why SketchUp is so great for asset design. SketchUp allows you to rough up a quick, low-poly model of virtually anything you can think of. Then, if you import it into your game and it fits in well with the overall design of the game, the game play, and the level, you can then decide whether to take the time to finesse the model to bring it up to par.

Now that you've got the basic form of your car, you can do two things:

- Refine the car's form step-by-step until you have a highly-refined model
- Create a highly-detailed and lifelike texture to simulate a highly-detailed model

The first of these is more suited to realistic photo rendering for such things as advertising or movies. The second is more suited to gaming. As I've mentioned previously, the game and movie industries are rapidly converging into one. We might soon find that both game and film assets require high-level details in both texturing and geometry (mesh).

Refining the car's geometry

The temptation now is to launch in and model everything that's possible to model before your car is complete. As I said before, that's a wrong way of going about it. You'll get discouraged. Besides, this is game-asset modeling, where "light is right." Keep your models light in detail, light in file size. Light is right!

Actually, your car is almost finished anyway. Or, at least the mesh is. There's just some obvious glitches in the mesh that we have to see to, and then we're done!

Time for action – sitting on the hood

The hood doesn't look right, does it? Let's fix that now. This is the complicated bit, because cars are complicated. Car bodies are not defined by the simple intersection of three forms that we've carried out just now. Cars want to be curvy! Curves are our enemy in SketchUp. Don't forget that SketchUp was initially designed for architects, and the nearest an architect ever gets to modeling curves is when they enter the annual RIBA fashion show for charity.

There used to be an advertisement going around where a guy made himself a VW Beetle lookalike from his old beat-up car, by getting an elephant to sit on the hood. Turns out this method is actually quite successful. I've chosen to show you how, in here. Remember, the model now represents the biggest dimension the car could get to, because you made it by tracing the very outside of the three car views. The real-life curved geometry of the car must sit somewhere within this outer box you've created. And here lies the beauty of this method. You can now keep working on it, or reducing it in size or form, until you get what you want. Easy! If an elephant can do it, so can you.

1. Select each image in turn, explode it, sample the texture, and paint it onto the car's geometry. Start with the side view and paint all the sides of the car.

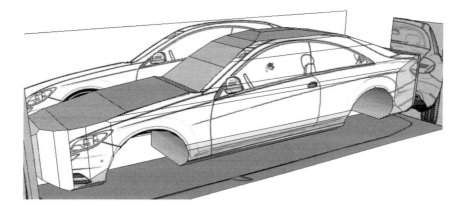

2. Follow with the plan, and finally the front and back view. It's up to you which geometry you paint with which texture.

3. Now, hide the texture images again. When you're done you should have something like the following screenshot:

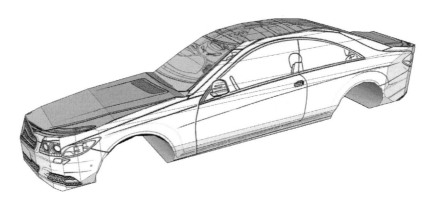

4. It immediately looks more like a car! We could stop modeling here and just add the texture. But have you noticed something's not quite right with the hood?

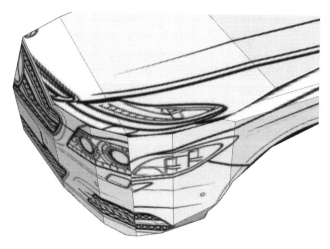

5. It looks real messed up. That's because we haven't got the curve in the hood right yet. Let's fix it now.

6. With the **Pencil** tool, draw along the line of the hood as it appears on the Plan view, as I've indicated here. Make sure your tooltip shows **On Edge** or **endpoint** each time you create a line, not **On Face**.

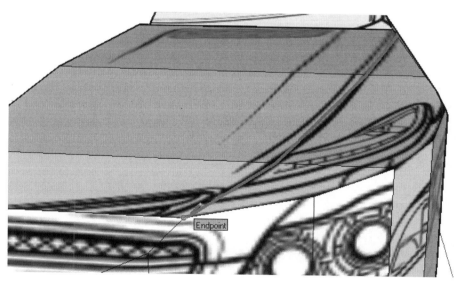

7. Now, draw along the line of the hood where it appears on the side view, as shown next.

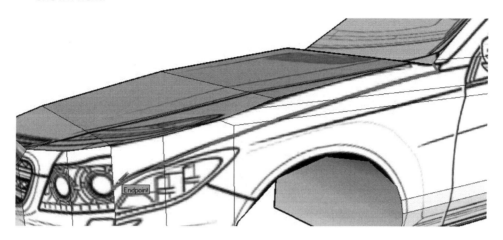

8. The funny thing is that both these lines should be the same line. See how they end just by the headlight in both the plan and side views? Let's fix it.

9. First use the **Erase** tool to delete everything in between the lines, as shown in the following screenshot. We now know none of this exists, so we're getting rid of it. Remember the elephant?

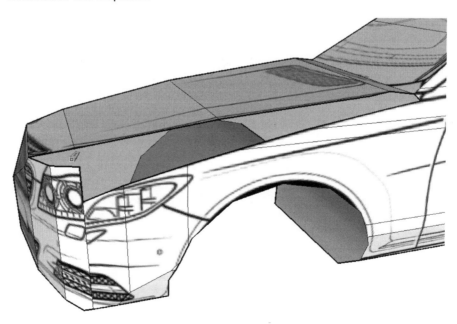

10. Because the geometry we have is the largest shape the car could attain, we know that the line at the centre of the hood is pretty much accurate (see next image). So, that has to stay as it is.

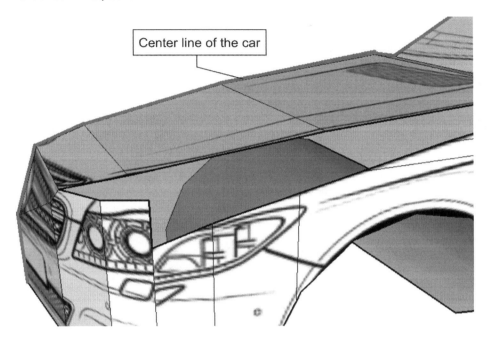

Center line of the car

11. We also know that the line we've drawn on the hood is accurate in the plan directions (Red and Green). So, it only has to move in the Blue direction. The line on the side view is accurate in the Blue axis, so we will use this as a guide.

12. Line up your view so that you're looking at the hood from the side, as shown in the following screenshot.

13. Use the **Move** tool and click on one of the endpoints on the edge of the hood. Press *Alt* once to operate the fold mode.

14. Remember that we simply need to move this point down in the Blue axis until it's at the same level as the other line. Make sure the axis line goes blue, and then hold *Shift* to keep movement locked to the Blue direction.

15. Now, click on the edge of the car, on the second line you drew, as shown next:

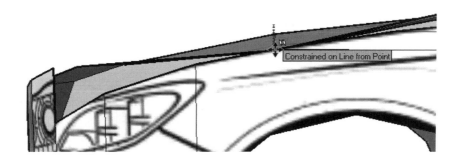

16. Repeat this with each endpoint along the line of the hood until you've pulled the whole line down to where it should be. You can see the result in the next image:

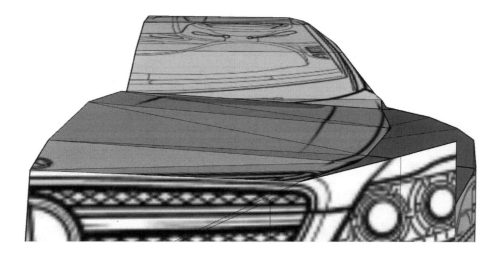

What just happened?

Every point in 3D space can be defined by a place in the red, blue, and green directions. To find any point in the geometry of our car, we need only to decide where these are on the plan, side, or end views. We decided by looking at the plan view that the red and green points were correct. This is always the case with a plan view. We simply needed to find the one missing—namely the blue one. The side view has the blue axis correct, so now we have all three. Having discovered this, you then drew the line correctly on the plan view, and modified the blue axis position of the line by referring to the side view. Phew!

This is how you can model anything in SketchUp, no matter how complicated it seems. All you need to do is draw a line correct in two axes, then move it in the direction (axis) you haven't got right yet.

Armed with this knowledge you're now entirely equipped to model's complex organic forms, namely the rest of this car! But before you do, let's patch up the hole we made just now.

Modeling by hand

There are often times when modeling with SketchUp that you have to resort to patching things up by hand. Patching things can be done quite easily with the Pencil tool.

There is only one rule for this: "Always stick to triangles."

When you select any three points in any space and then join them up, you always get a flat surface. When you draw lines defining a flat surface in SketchUp, it turns it into a face. Always draw triangles and you can't go wrong! Do not deviate from this rule to try to be clever, because you'll probably regret it.

Time for action – applying a car body filler with the pencil tool

1. First, let's draw around the headlight to get rid of that ugly bit sticking up. Follow the approximate line of the grille and headlight as shown in the following screenshot:

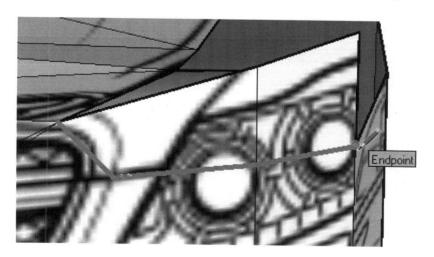

2. Erase the upper part above your line.

3. The car folds on another line slightly further down the side view as shown in the next image. Draw a line along this line and again erase everything above it.

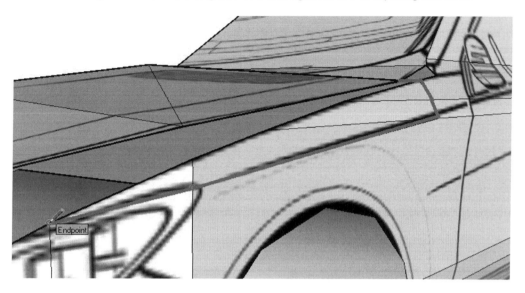

4. You now have an even bigger hole, but at least you know everything that's there now is more or less correct. Now it's time to do the patching.

5. Using pencil lines, just make triangles between the two edges of the hole, just like the example I've shown here.

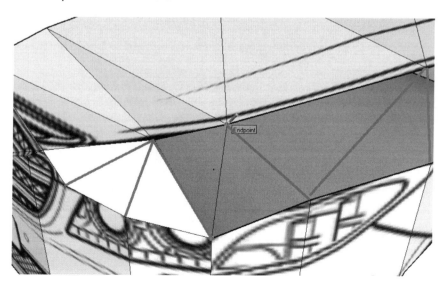

6. Before you know it you'll have the car patched up. When you paint the front view back onto the geometry, it all looks much, much better.

What just happened?

First, we found the line on the side of the car where the bodywork starts to fold into the hood. We then drew that line and connected it with the edge of the hood using several lines made with the **Pencil** tool into the triangular faces. This filled in the surface between the line on the hood and the line on the side.

Have a go hero — reinvent the wheel

Now it's your turn. Unhide the side view image and create a wheel on it using the **Circle** tool, then project the texture onto it, **push/pull**, and copy it around the car.

Now that your mesh is all but done, let's take a good look at what you have achieved. To gain an idea of how good this geometry can really look like, even without texturing, do the following:

1. Delete the face in the middle of the car.
2. Select the car body and turn it into a component.
3. Copy it and flip the component. Now, stick it back together.
4. Select both and then right-click and select **Soften Edges**.

5. If you have a rendering application installed, turn on shadows now and render. If not, download the **ShaderLight** free version (`http://www.artvps.com/index.php/downloads/try_shaderlight`). Just click on the camera button to start rendering.

Creating the car texture from photos

In this section, you're going to discover how to texture your car. Or, to be more precise, rediscover what you know. , because, surprisingly perhaps, texturing a car is just the same as texturing any of the other things you already made. If that wasn't good enough news, then I can tell you that you already did most of the hard work when you set up the orthographic views in the first place. All you need to do now is:

1. Open up your original file in GIMP.

2. Find (or take) some photos of your car.

3. Paste them over the top of the line drawings of the front, top, side and back.

6. Stretch them a bit.

7. Smudge them around like you did with the wrench in *Chapter 7, Quick Standard Assets*.

8. Reload the image into SketchUp.

And as if by magic, your textured car will appear!

Finding car images

Finding well photographed car images can be difficult, because you need several views of the same car. The best thing to do is either get them from professional texturing sites, or take them yourself.

 The manufacturer's website will often contain excellent images, often including near-Orthographic views, too. Use these to practice with, but don't upload them to 3D-Warehouse, even if your car is just one part of a larger model. These images are copyrighted.

Some websites with car textures

- `http://www.textures.es3dstudios.com`
- `http://freetextures.3dtotal.com`
- `http://www.turbosquid.com`

Type `car texture` into the search box and you'll find hundreds of them for around $5 each.

Taking your own car images

Finding cars to photograph is actually far easier than it sounds; they're everywhere! You don't need to find a friend with the car you want and ask them for permission. The fact is, people leave cars lying around all the time. You'll have the best luck in big parking lots. Here's how to get some good photos:

- Wait for an overcast day
- Borrow the best camera and telephoto lens that you can
- Find a car that you like, with plenty of space around it
- Stand as far away as possible to take your shots, so that distortion is minimized
- Kneel so that your camera is level with the top of the hood
- Take the front, side and rear views
- Take a few close-ups of the badge, lights, and wheels

When you're done with your texture, you can sell it on TurboSquid, too.

Find a friend in the trade

For the purposes of our tutorial, I found the texture using a third method. I phoned someone in the car industry at www.thecarspy.net who agreed to allow us to use their photos. Find their photos on Flickr.com by going to: http://www.flickr.com/photos/thecarspy/sets/. The photo set you might be particularly interested in is the 2007 Mercedes Benz CL63 which bears a striking (if not perfect) resemblance to your SketchUp model. When you open up the set, you will see a plethora of car views and details. You can download the ones you need and give credit to the copyright owner in your work.

Time for action

1. Open your MB_Master.xcf GIMP file

2. Go to **Image ¦ Mode ¦ RGB**. This turns the image into a color image.

3. Go to **File ¦ Open** as layers and select all your car images. Click on **Open**.

4. The images will open as layers in your GIMP project. Hide all of them except the base layer and the front view.

5. Drag the front view image under the front view drawing.

6. Drag from the ruler at the side to create a ruler at each side of the car drawing, as shown next:

7. Select the image layer and move it to line up with one of the rulers. Select the **Scale** tool and click once on the image.

8. Select the **Chain** icon.

9. Use the scale grips on the image to resize the car to fit to the rulers as you can see next:

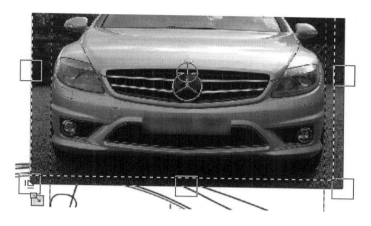

10. Click on **Scale** when you're done.

11. Use the **Crop** tool as you've done in previous chapters, and crop out the left half of the car and anything above the hood. Select the current layer only.

12. Reduce the opacity of the layer a little and change the layer mode to Multiply. You can now see the two images superimposed.

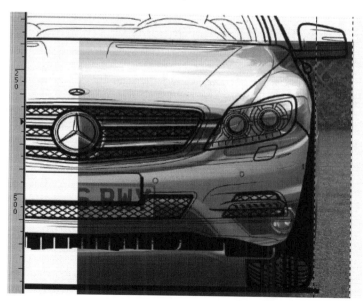

13. Use the **Perspective** tool to stretch the car out if needed.

14. Load the same, or a different front view as a layer again, and move into place for the windshield.

15. Move the layer below the previous one in the layers pallet, and change the **opacity** and **Mode** as before.

16. Use rulers for the top and bottom of the windshield and scale the image.

17. Now use a layer mask to show some more of the second image through where shown in the next image sequence.

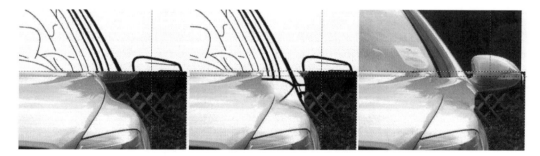

18. Crop the second image layer like you did with the first.

19. You should now have something like the following screenshot

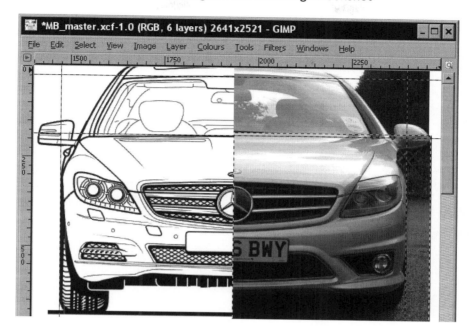

What just happened?

Orthographic drawings depict the world without perspective. Things don't get smaller the further they are away from you. Cameras do. So when you pasted your photo over the orthographic drawing, you had some problems. If you got the front of the car the right size, the windshield looked too small. If you had the windshield right, the front would look too big. What you've done to solve this problem is use two copies of the image stacked one on top of the other. One is scaled to the windshield, and one to the front of the car. You then used a layer mask to modify where you wished each of these two images to show. As you can see from the previous screenshot, it works quite well!

The layers in your layer pallet should look like this:

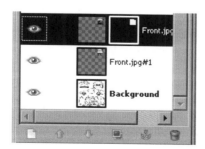

Save a copy of your texture image and load it into SketchUp like you did before. Your car now updates with the photo texture on the front.

Painting in individual elements

I now want to show you another technique. one that gives you far more control. It also takes a little more time to set up, but you can recoup this time in the end. This technique is a lot less frustrating than the previous one, as you might have discovered already!

Time for action – painting over the rear view

1. Start just like before and import your rear view image as a layer. This time rather than setting up the rulers to the sides of the car, set them up to the edges of the lights (on the orthographic drawing).

2. Scale the photo so that the edge of the lights line up with the rulers.

3. Set up a Layer Mask for the photo layer, and check the box that says Black (full transparency).

4. Get a brush, increase its size in the brush pallet, and paint the main parts of the trunk and lights, as you can see next:

5. Switch this layer off. Move the rulers to the top and bottom of the rear window and scale a new copy of the image.

6. Use the **Scale** tool to reduce the layer from side to side.

7. Use a mask and reveal just the rear window. It should look something like this:

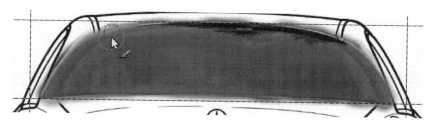

8. You can see by now that this method gives you far better control. When you switch on the previous layer, you will see that they blend seamlessly.

9. Move the rulers to the side of the car and scale a new copy of the image.

10. Move the layer into position using the Mercedes logo to center it, and the line of the bumper to get the height right.

11. Repeat the layer masking process. You should end up with the following:

What just happened?

This is a much more accurate and controlled way of texturing. You've taken discreet elements of the car photo, resized them, and painted them onto the base drawing. This has allowed you to retain control over what goes where, and scale the photo much more accurately to the drawing. The second benefit is that you have a complete image, rather than just one side of the car.

Have a go hero

Now it's your turn to use this same technique on the side view of your car.

Ignore the wheels. We will be doing those separately later.

Time for action – creating blend areas

You now have all the important elements of the car textured. All you have left to do is make sure the different views work together properly:

1. Create a new layer and name it **Blend**.

2. Move the Blend layer just above the Background layer in the layer pallet.

2. Select the **Colour Picker** tool from the main pallet. Now, select the features as shown in the next screenshot:

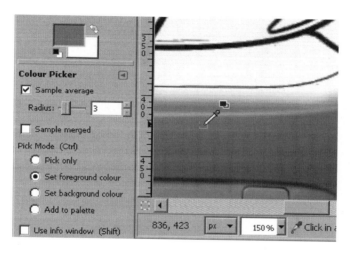

4. Select the layer containing the car bumper, then click on a light area of color on the bumper as you can see here.

5. Now that you have selected your color, select the **Blend** layer and select the **Fill** tool.

6. Click on anywhere in the image to fill the layer with the color you sampled.

Create a blend layer from images

Even better, find an image that shows a flat area of paintwork without any reflections and create a tiled image out of it. Make it the same size as your current image, and Insert this instead of the Blend layer. You learned how to do all of this in *Chapter 5, Game Levels in SketchUp*.

7. Use your layer masks to fade out all the edges of your images. This has the effect of painting in the same color as your paintwork..

8. Take special care to reach the areas where the front, side, or rear view textures join adjacent textures, such as the frames round the windows.

9. Now, reduce the opacity of your brush to 30 and go around again, blending the edges into the background gradually. You should have something roughly like the following:

10. Load it into SketchUp to see what the car looks like now:

What just happened?

Your car's coming along nicely. You're almost there! There are now no more white areas on your car. You've taken care of it by creating a blanket cover of grey paint to hide any transitions.

Have a go hero

You can see from the previous rendering, and probably from your own model, that in several places the transition doesn't work yet. These transitions (like the one in the next image) fall along the lines of SketchUp faces where you decided to paint the front, rear, or side texture. It's now your job to add extra lines onto your SketchUp model in the best places to join one texture to another. It's then a matter of trial and error to get your texture to match. The main idea is to have two adjoining areas of texture that have the grey background color.

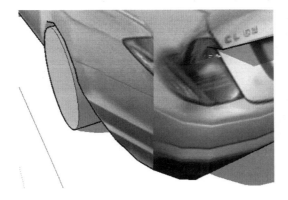

Here's the modified geometry:

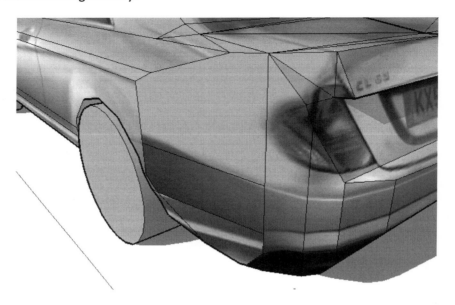

UV unwrap plugins

One of the next steps in becoming a game asset guru involves getting to grips with **UV unwrapping**, which allows you to select some faces and create a single texture map for those faces. This will allow you to blend one area into another seamlessly. There are several plugins available:

- `http://www.unwrap3d.com/u3d/downloads. aspx`

  Just select the SketchUp plugin and download as shown:

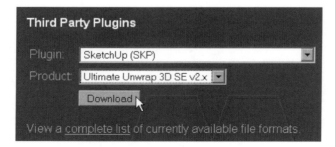

- The UTV toolkit (`http://tinyurl.com/UV-toolkit`)
- Tgi3D SU Amorph Training Edition (`http://www.tgi3d.com/index. php?Page=Download`).

Have a go hero – UV tools

Try out Ultimate Unwrap 3D or Tgi3D and fix the texture on your car. Do this by selecting the faces involving the blend area and creating a texture for those faces using the UV tool:

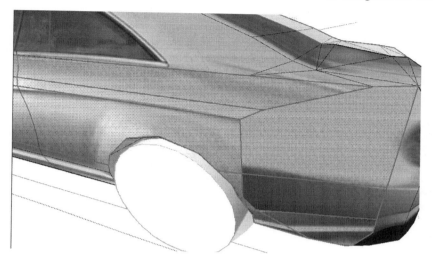

With Tgi3D this is done by right-clicking and then selecting **Create texture**. After you do that, a pop-up window will show where you will enter the following values:

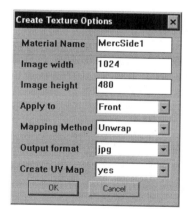

Then select the new texture in the **Materials Pallet** and edit it in GIMP:

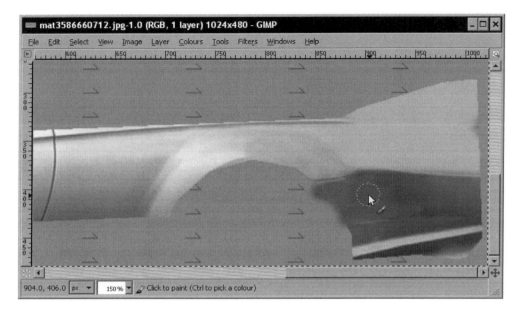

Time for action – how realistic wheels make all the difference

1. Back in GIMP, reveal the front wheel of your side view with the **Layer Masks** on those layers.

2. Save a copy of the new image.

3. Reload it in SketchUp as before.

4. You should now have four realistic wheels.

What just happened?

I told you the wheels make all the difference.

Summary

We've come a long way in a very short time. In this chapter, you have learned how to create a car from some photos and some blueprints taken from the Internet. You've achieved a low-polygon sporty automobile for your games using only simple tricks and techniques. I'm afraid this is as far as you can go using these shortcut methods. To get any further in terms of realism, you now need to either export your model to Blender and learn how to create UV maps for your texture, or gradually add in more detail piece by piece. Once you have a detailed model, you can apply non-photo materials and render it for greater realism.

Of course, for a really stunning vehicle you also need to model the interior and the occupant, but those are a topic for another book. Who knows, now you've caught the SketchUp bug, maybe you'll end up writing it.

In this chapter, you learned how to:

- Model from orthographic 2D drawings
- Create a quick approximate form by intersecting three views
- Start refining the model by moving geometry one axis at a time
- Apply photo textures to your orthographic views for automatic projection onto your car model
- Layer up photos to get rid of camera depth of field
- Fill in the texturing gaps with Blend layers

...and lots more. In the end you were left with a car. You showed it to your mom, and this time she said...

"You did that? I don't believe it!"

Your feeling of self-worth was restored and you both lived happily ever after. The End.

9

The Main Building - Inside and Out

After four days without food, water, sleep, or seeing another living soul, you're finally nearing your mission's end. It has been a grueling challenge of survival. Your body is shaking constantly. Your vision is blurred. Your eyes hurt and your head pounds. Your tongue sticks to the roof of your mouth. Ahead, you can see a clearing. Something inside you makes you certain this is what you have been searching for. You emerge from the undergrowth and stumble towards the ramshackle building at the center of the clearing, prise the doors open and look inside towards your prize, the end of your bitter struggle, when...

"Honey, we're home. Where are you?"

There are footsteps on the stairs and your bedroom door flies open.

"It looks like you haven't moved from your bedroom for days! Have you been playing that game again?"

In this chapter, you will be setting up the final objective. It's up to you what it is, but make it good. Your game players will want something worth staying up all night for. Or all week. You have to compete with food, sleep, and friends.

When you craft the climax to your game level only you can decide what it will be. It takes imagination and skill, and these are two things this book can only introduce you to! Crafting levels, designing exciting areas to explore, dreaming up artifacts to find, and puzzles to solve is what you will be doing from now on after you graduate from this Beginner's Guide. It's almost time to let you out into the wide, wild world of game asset and level design.

Before we part company, there's a couple of things we can still do together. First, there's the wrapping to the present that lies within the clearing. The building within which you will place your final goal. Your goal can be a spaceship that the hero flies away in, or one that contains a toxic alien. It can be a bunch of criminals sat around a card table that you have to take out one by one. It can be a rare artifact you have to escape with using stealth tactics. Anything! It's all up to you—now that you have the skills to accomplish it.

In this chapter, you will practice:

- Texturing a building from photo materials
- Creating a lifelike building from scratch
- Arranging all your assets into your completed game level in Unity
- Setting up ambient lighting, sky and fog.
- Adding a realistic city skyline as a distant backdrop
- Creating an executable file or web page for your completed game level

What you will have at the end of this chapter is a file that you can burn to disc, e-mail around, or upload to the Web. A real 3D game anyone can play. That's the prize for you at the end of my game level.

Creating the main building

This following figure is the main industrial building at the center of your game level. It's simple and looks pretty authentic. Before you ask—no, I didn't paint that sign—it's there on the actual photo! Let's create the building now:

Time for action – clipping round textures

1. Just like before, let's find the textures we need on CGTextures.com. The one you want is within **Buildings ¦ Industrial**.

2. Download the large one. Here it is:

3. Open it up in GIMP and select a large rectangular area, the full height of the building, containing only the metal cladding panels.

4. Using what you learned in the previous chapters, create a seamless texture for the side of the building. You should end up with something like the one shown next:

5. If you want to be really clever, resize the canvas of the first texture and add this new texture to it. This will also leave space for further textures for the roof and interior.

6. You might have something like the image shown here.

7. Now, copy the layer containing the front of the building. Place the copy below the original one.

8. Now use the **Clone** tool to paint over the sign of the copy.

9. Use **Save a Copy** to save your completed texture as a **PNG** file.

10. Find a suitable roof material on CGTextures.com and turn it into a tile-able texture if it isn't tile-able already.

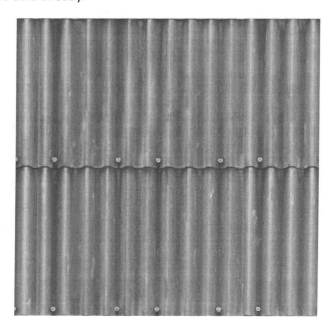

11. In SketchUp, import the texture of the building using the **Import as Image** setting, and resize it with the **Tape Measure Tool**. The full width of the front of the building should be about 20m.

12. Set the image upright and draw around the front of the building. Alternatively, draw around it with the texture lying down, then put it upright afterwards.

13. **Push/Pull** the building until it's 18m deep (you will adjust this with **Push/Pull** to fit the side texture in *Step 19*).

14. Now explode the image. Use the **Sample Paint** tool to sample the image and paint it onto the front face of the building.

15. Erase the rest of the image. You should have the following:

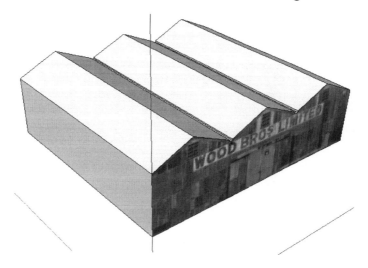

16. Place the bottom left-hand side corner onto the **Origin** using the **Move** tool.

 You can get this file from the download pack named Chapter8_ IndustrialBuilding_01.skp.

17. Texture the sides of your building by selecting your new material in the **In Model** tab of the **Materials** pallet, and then painting it on the left-hand side.

18. Move and scale the texture as necessary from within the right-click menu.

19. Repeat with the opposite side. **Push/Pull** the back face of the building to fit the texture if you need to.

20. Create a new material and load up the **Roofing Plates** texture, as shown in the next screenshot:

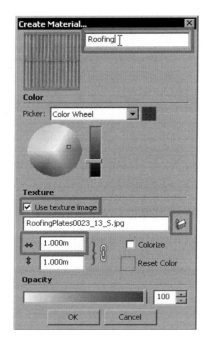

21. Type in a material name and set the scale as required. You may change this number a few times until it looks right in the model.

22. Paste the new texture onto the roof.

23. Sample the front and paint it onto the back. Notice the sign's the wrong way around? This is why you created a separate back texture. Move this into place now.

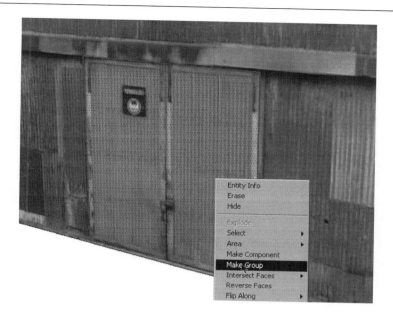

24. Draw a rectangle around the door, select it, right-click and select **Make Group**.

25. Use the **Move** tool to copy the door away from the building. Now, **Explode** the group that's left on the building face.

26. Use the **Push/Pull** tool to create a corridor as shown next:

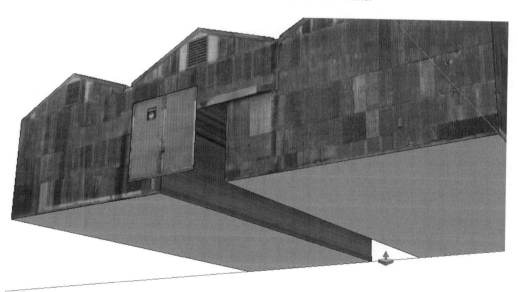

27. Create Rectangles for both leaves of the door and group each one (into two groups). Now, double-click on each group to edit it and **Push/Pull** each into shape as shown here.

28. Move them aside to open the doors.

29. Move them back against the face of the building.

30. Now, create a rectangle on the face above the door. **Push/Pull** it out a little further than the doors as you can see here.

31. Do this on both the front and back of the building.

32. Now copy the doors to the other side of the building and close them. We want the player to have to go right around the building before they can gain entry.

Modeling the interior

Now, it's time to move our attention to the inside of a building for the first time. Here's an easy way to quickly model corridors and rooms inside your building.

1. Move your view so that you can see under the building.

2. Select any tile material and paint it onto the three sides of the corridor.

3. Now use the **Rectangle** tool and create an opening as you can see next. Use the **Push/Pull** tool to carve out a corridor, alcove, or room.

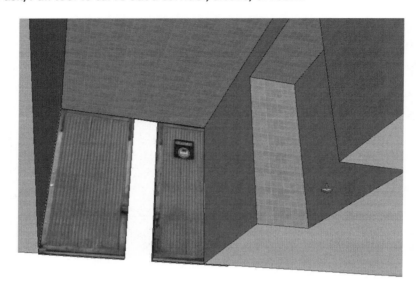

4. Simply repeat again and again, as you can see next.

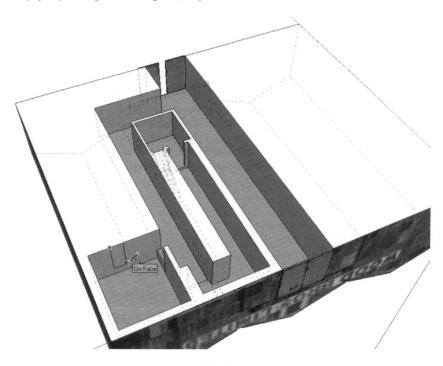

What just happened?

You've just learned how to create a fairly complex building with external and internal features and texturing. You made the doors as separate groups so that these can be animated in Unity (or any other game development environment) later. The reason you turned your building upside down to model the interior is that this method is just so easy to use. You can fluidly (and admittedly, fairly randomly) experiment with rooms, corridors, stairs, alcoves, and the likes. Literally, all you have to do is draw a line from top to bottom whenever you wish to create a bend in the corridor. All you have to do is make a rectangle (as you can see me doing in the previous image) to create a new door and room. It's "subtractive modeling," which forces you to work with the space you have. This is actually what happens in real life — you only have so much room in a building.

Have a go hero

How you finish the inside of your building is up to you. It's as simple as carving out your upside-down world with rectangles and **Push/Pull**, then texturing using the techniques you have learned already. Take a deep breath, pull your stomach in and puff out your chest, straighten your back, and salute. You're a genuine hero now. Go to work.

Your final 3D game level in Unity 3D

We're nearing the end of your game. In the next few pages you will:

- Gather all your assets into one SketchUp file and rearrange your level just as you like it
- Create a background skyline
- Export the finished level and import it into Unity
- Set up the see through (Alpha channel) textures
- Make final adjustments to your lighting
- Install your first-person controller
- Test the game
- Export the game to web format for others to play
- Create an executable file of your game

Time for action – setting up a playable game level layout

1. Using the terrain you have created or the one provided in the download pack, insert your main building onto the flat plan above the terrain, right in the square you allocated for it.

2. Now use **File ¦ Import** to bring in more of the contextual buildings you created in *Chapter 7, Quick Standard Assets*, once you have cleaned them up from the 3D Warehouse, made them from photos or taken them from the download pack.

3. Place them where you want them in the level—but not on the terrain—on the flat plan. You might get something like this:

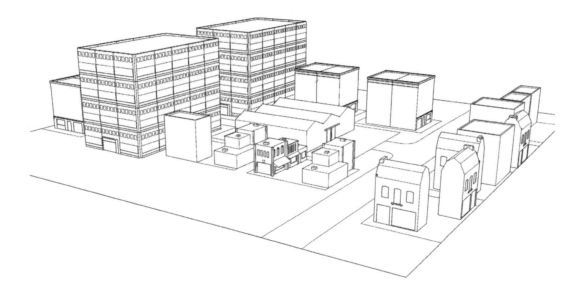

Increasing computer speed

When you're dealing with a large number of models in one SketchUp scene and you find that your computer system is slowing down, you can use the monochrome view style to make everything faster. That's because SketchUp doesn't have to worry about sending texture information to your screen, which frees up your computer's memory.

4. When you're happy where everything is, move each building down onto the terrain individually using **Move** and locking to the Blue axis as shown here.

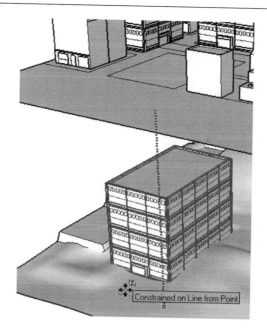

5. After dropping each building down, check that the whole building footprint is poking through the terrain by looking at the building from the underside:

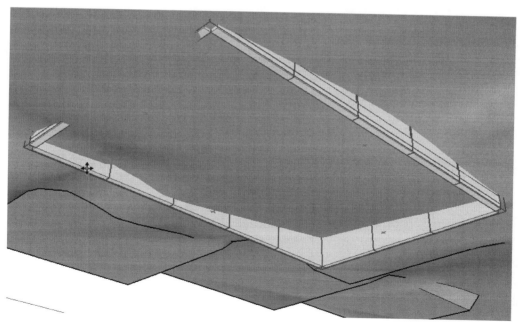

6. As you can see in the previous screenshot, the left-hand side of the building is still partly above the terrain. You can now either move the building down further, edit the terrain to make it higher at that point, or extend that part of the building downward.

7. The rest of our building looks absolutely fine partly buried in the ground, as you can see to the right of the image, and the windows are well above ground level, so in this case I'll just drop the building down a little so that the door touches the terrain.

8. In the case of the next one, lots of the windows are ending up getting covered, so let's put the building on top of a retaining wall. To edit a building in-situ, it's best to select **View ¦ Component Edit ¦ Hide Rest Of Model**.

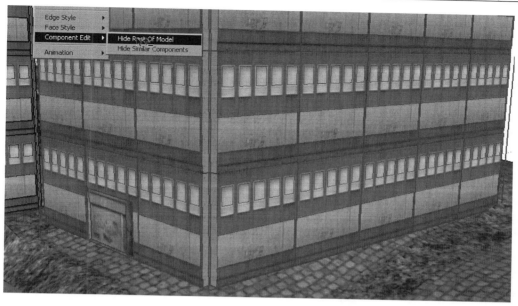

9. It's now possible to double-click on the component to edit it, and you'll have a blank canvas to do it in.

10. Do this now with one of your buildings. Now use the Rectangle tool to create a flat base underneath and **Push/Pull** it into shape.

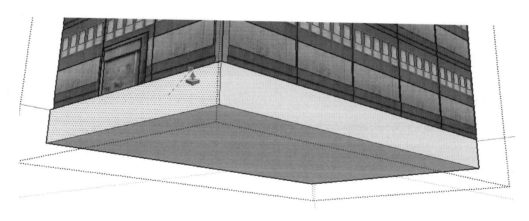

11. Go to the **Materials** pallet and select an industrial looking brick from **Brick and Cladding**. Hopefully, you installed the extra materials pack from *Chapter 2, Tools that Grow on Trees*, so you have a good range to choose from. Paste the texture onto all surfaces.

12. It looks truly awful as you can see here. But I can assure you, retaining walls are more often than not awful in real life too!

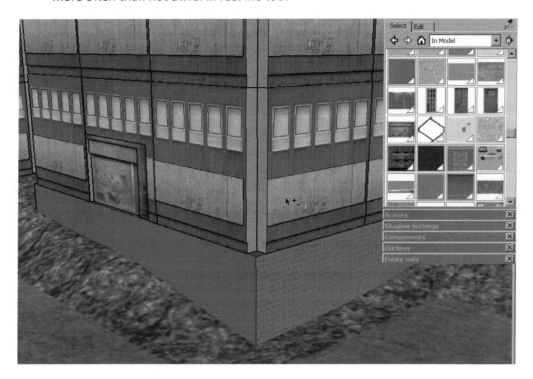

What just happened?

Our level appears to be going from bad to worse. First, we had to half bury a building, and now we're having to put it on top of a hideous wall! It's that blasted hilly terrain's fault.

There's nothing else for it. We're going to have to make the terrain nice and flat so that we can continue un-interrupted.

Not so fast! Let's think about this for a minute. If you were the architect of this building, what would you do? Well, look at the thing, will you? It's a concrete monstrosity. No architect went anywhere near that thing. It was put together after the 2nd world war when utility was the order of the day. So, yes, it's ugly, but ask yourself this question: Is ugly an exception, or a rule?

Level-led design

Now we're getting somewhere. Ugly is (most of the time) a rule, not an exception. If you want a realistic game world then you're going to have to embrace the concept of "ugly." What this terrain is actually doing for us is forcing us to compromise on our neat design plan and actually make it live. We are having to botch things up, make a compromise, and add in ugly patchwork details, just as in real life. In fact, this is leading us down avenues that will make the game better—more real—without us even having to think too hard. The game level is leading us to better design. All we have to do is react to what it is asking of us.

Have a go hero – what would I do if I were an Architect?

Now's your chance to start experimenting. Notice in the previous screenshot that there are several doors, shutters, and metal textures already in the model. We can utilize these to our advantage and just let the level lead us where it wants to go. Ask yourself, what would the architect or builder do here? Notice the following things:

- The door is now inaccessible. How will people get to it?
- The walls are bare. What would a young person with plenty of time on his/her hands think about that situation?
- What's behind the wall? Did the builder think about putting a basement or utility room inside?
- Could the office workers be parking down there? If they could, do they need air or are they just going to have to hold their breath? What about car fumes?

In asking yourself these questions, you will come naturally to the answers. They don't have to be the answers—just a bunch of answers. Then, go ahead and model it as if you were building it. You can see my attempt when you open the model Chapter 9's `Final.skp` from the download pack.

Time for action – digging out a terrain

When you created your terrain, you stamped rectangles onto it in case you wanted to remove them later. Have a go at this now:

1. Select an area where you would like your buildings to be lower down—perhaps you've placed buildings there and the area is just too hilly.

2. Go to **View** and select **View Hidden Geometry**.

3. Now, edit the terrain and use the **Erase** tool on the rectangle as shown next:

4. You can remove all of it, or as much as you want.

5. When you're done, drop a blue line down one corner as shown in the next screenshot, and then join it up to all other corners, making sure you stick to the Red, Green, and Blue axes only.

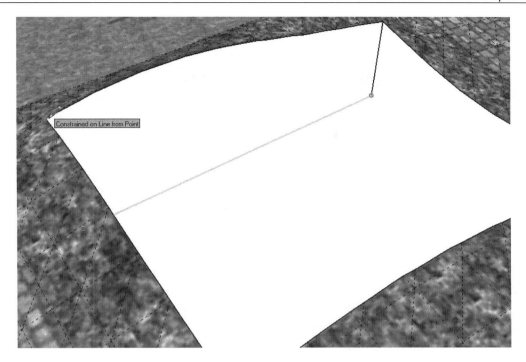

6. Draw vertical lines up at each corner. You should finish up with a rectangular hole.

7. You can now **Push/Pull** the base up as high as it will go and paste a texture in there.

8. Place the buildings in the hole.

What just happened?

First of all, you used your modeling skills to delete the area that you stamped out in *Chapter 5, Game Levels in SketchUp*, then to manually recreate faces with the pencil tool until you had filled in the gaps. You can see four of the five faces you created in the previous image. Remember, if you stick to drawing lines in the Red, Green, and Blue axes you will usually be able to create planar (flat) boundaries with your **Pencil** tool which will fill in with a face automatically.

Your final level might look something like this:

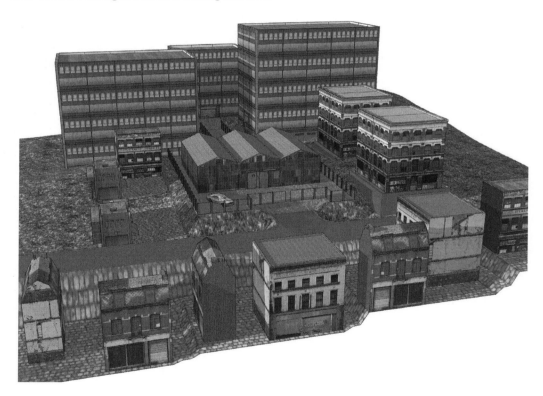

Have a go Hooligan

Can you see any large areas of brickwork? If this were your town, would it still look this clean? Empty spaces such as these are just inviting you to spray-paint your name and logo all over them. If you've never been a hooligan before, now's the opportunity of a lifetime!

Find a surface and right-click, and then select **Make Unique Texture**. Use **Edit Texture** to open it in GIMP—and let rip with the **Air Brush** tool!

Time for action – exporting buildings to Unity 3D

1. It's now time to export to Unity. First open Unity and check what you already have inside.

2. In SketchUp, select the buildings you just inserted. Now, group them and label the group `SU_Buildings`.

3. Follow the steps in Chapter 5, *Game Levels in SketchUp*, to export this group to your **SketchUp4Games** folder. Remember to select **Export only current selection**.

4. When you switch to Unity, your buildings will load automatically, but they won't be in the right place yet.

Using temporary 3D Warehouse assets in your games

Importing these buildings to Unity may take a long time if you used buildings from the 3D Warehouse. That's because people uploading buildings to 3D Warehouse aren't always thinking about low polygon modeling, using a single texture, or other game asset performance issues. Don't worry about this. Don't forget that at this stage it's all about getting a playable level into Unity so that you can test it and decide what artistic or gameplay decisions to take next. If and when you start to finalize your game, you will also wish to replace these assets with ones you made yourself or other people's you fixed up really well for game use (see *Chapter 7, Quick Standard Assets*).

5. Open the **Project** tab, and click on **OuterBuildings**. Select the **Generate Colliders** check box and change **Scale Factor** to **1**.

6. Drag your new asset into the model window.

7. Your buildings will appear somewhere in your game level, but not necessarily where you want them to be!

8. Next, select the group and type in **0** in each of the x, y, and z dimension boxes. Hit *Enter*.

9. Your buildings will move into place.

10. Now, check that all textures have imported correctly. If you notice any see-through faces, such as in the next image, that will be because these are back faces in SketchUp (see *Chapter 7, Quick Standard Assets*). Go back into SketchUp and reverse these faces before continuing, and then re-import.

11. In SketchUp, select all the fence components, group them, and import them into Unity (select "two-sided faces" in the **Export** options this time). Follow the steps above to resize and put them in the right place.

12. Now, import one of each of your assets and place them somewhere in your SketchUp level, then export to Unity. You should have one each of the following:

- ° Pallets
- ° Oil drums
- ° The wrench
- ° Cars
- ° Any additional street furniture you've modeled or imported
- ° The main building
- ° Import any furniture and other items for the inside of the building individually if the game requires them to move or be interacted with (for example, opening doors).

13. In Unity, move the lights and pallets you placed there in *Chapter 6, Importing to a professional game application: Unity 3D,* to where you want them, now that you've designed your main building.

14. You can copy your assets by selecting them and going to **Edit ⦙ Duplicate**. Put plenty of barrels and pallets around the place. Use the Rotate button to make them look more randomly placed.

What just happened?

When you export a group of SketchUp objects, that group will also act as one group in Unity. This is fine for static elements such as buildings and fences, but you need something to move, such as a door opening and closing or a barrel rolling over when you kick it, it's best to import it individually. The reason you imported a single item instead of many of them (for example, in case of a barrel, you should have many of them scattered around) is that you can assign scripts and physical attributes to the single unit in Unity, and then copy that item around. Copying items within a game development environment such as Unity, rather than SketchUp, is much more memory-efficient because game engines can recognize when an object is just a copy of another. These are called **Instances**. This means that only one version of the object is loaded into the memory, and all other copies (instances) are not really there, but mirrors of the first one.

Rather, it's like putting up a few mirrors in front of you. You see yourself many times—but you don't need to eat any more. That's how you know these extra "YOUs" are just instances of you and not copies. If, however, you get downstairs tomorrow morning and all the Weetabix is gone, the people sitting at your breakfast table are definitely not instances. You should see a psychiatrist, or someone who can explain parallel universes to you. Or, maybe both.

Creating context with skyline and background terrain

Go to CGTextures.com and type in "skyline" into the search box. Download the `Landscapes0219` texture. You are now ready to create a background out of it, and will learn how to create alpha channels too for see-through textures.

Time for action – creating see-through textures

1. Open the skyline texture in GIMP. Use the **Fuzzy Select** tool to select the sky.

2. Click several times if you need to.

3. Go to **Layer ⦙ Transparency ⦙ Add Alpha channel**.

4. Now click on **Delete** or go to **Edit ¦ Clear**.

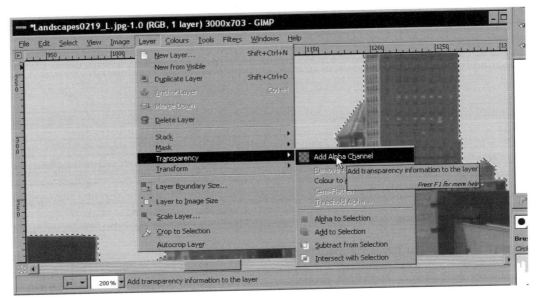

5. Go to **Layer ¦ Transform ¦ Offset** and offset the image by 1500 in X as shown next. This will wrap the edges round to the center.

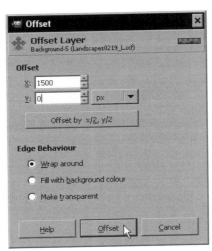

6. Now, use the **Clone** tool or **Smudge** tool to make the center seem seamless.

7. You should have something like the following. Save this as a PNG file named `Backdrop_Skyline`.

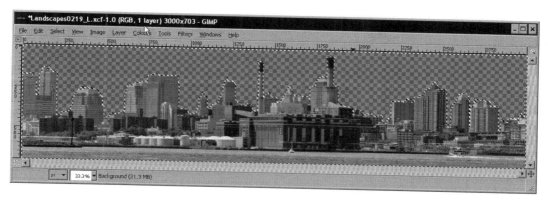

What just happened?

You created an Alpha channel which defines which pixels are see-through, and which are visible. You then made the sky area see-through so that you will be able to see the sky through it in Unity. You made the image seamless so that it can wrap around a cylinder or square.

Time for action – creating a backdrop

1. Back in SketchUp, create a large square centered in the terrain but much bigger than the terrain.

2. **Push/Pull** it upwards as you can see next. Delete the top face. **Push/Pull** the bottom face so that it sits below the terrain.

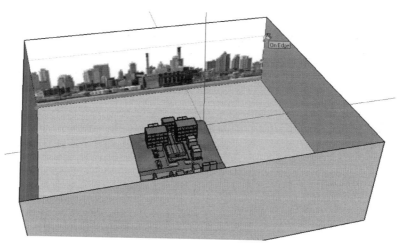

3. Reverse the face so that the white (front) face is towards the inside.

4. Import the background image as a texture, and click on the bottom left corner of one of the sides. Then, click on the other edge as you can see in the previous image.

5. Sample the texture and paste on all three other faces.

6. Find an interesting large scale texture and past it onto the bottom face.

7. Select all four top edges and move them up or down to get the full height of the image in.

8. You might have something like this. Save it and export to Unity:

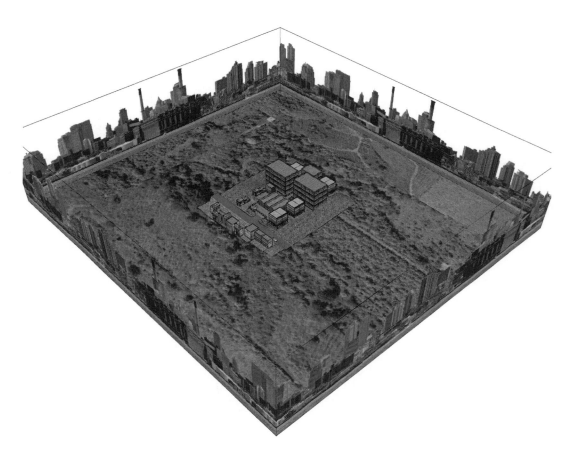

Trees and foliage are usually created within the game development environment, and Unity is no exception. Read all about the Unity Tree creator at http://unity3d.com/support/documentation/Components/class-Tree.html.

Time for action – enabling see-through materials (Alpha Channel)

Your fencing automatically shows correctly as a wire mesh in SketchUp. However, in Unity this needs setting up:

1. In the **Heirarchy** tab, click the little arrow next to **Fencing**, and then **Fencing Left**.

2. Select any of the fence components and select the mesh material as shown next:

3. Now, go to the **Shader** button, click on it, and select **Transparent ¦ Bumped Diffuse** or **Transparent ¦ Cutout**.

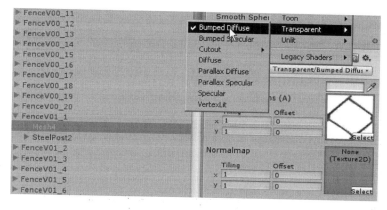

4. Your fence panels now look correct. Repeat this for any other fence panel textures.

What just happened?

You've told Unity that the Alpha channel saved with the texture should be used to clip the texture. Now, go ahead and do the same with the Skyline texture.

Time for action – enabling a skybox

Now we want to make the environment a little more real. Unity comes with a few **Skyboxes** that you can use straight out of the box. A Skybox is like being inside an upturned box with a sky painted on the inside. Crude but effective! Here's how to get one set up:

1. Go to **Edit ¦ Render settings**. The following pallet appears.

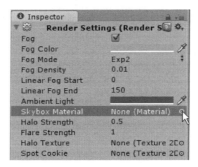

2. Select the dot next to the **Skybox Material**. A material selection pallet appears.

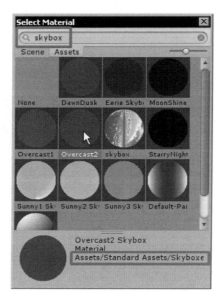

3. Type in skybox and select one of the thumbnails. Check whether the text at the bottom shows **Assets/Standard Assets/Skybox**, which is where the bundled Skyboxes are kept.

4. Now just close the pallet. Your sky appears next time you press **Play** in the **Game tab**.

Have a go hero - fog

If you chose one of the murkier skyboxes, you might also wish to introduce some fog to set off the atmosphere. This is accessed from the **Render settings** pallet. Enter a **Fog Density**, **Linear Fog Start,** and **Linear Fog End**. I suggest you just experiment with this.

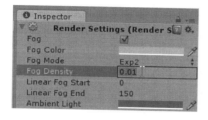

Time for action – ambient light

You already learned how to set up lights in Unity in *Chapter 6, Importing to a professional game application: Unity 3D*. That's the correct way of doing it for the most accuracy and realism. In order to get started more quickly though, you can set the level of ambient light. Ambient light is a term referring to the amount of light that's kind of just there. You don't see where it's coming from, so it casts no shadows; it's pretty boring, but it does the trick. Why not use it now to get up and running, and add more realistic lighting when you get the time?

1. Make sure you're in the **Game** tab.

2. Click on the **Ambient light** color bar. A color swatch appears as you can see in the next screenshot.

3. Select the level and color of light. The level is controlled by how far up or down you go. The color is selected by the bar on the right, and how far left to right you go.

4. If you want white light, just stay on the left and you'll be grand.

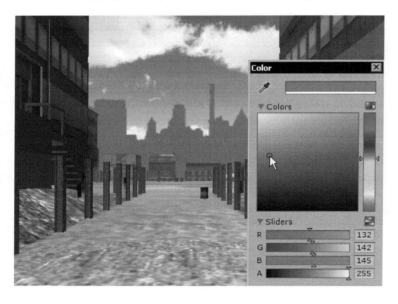

What just happened?

That's all folks! You've set up your environment and you're ready to rock and roll.

Exporting your game for others to play

Fame and fortune as a games designer or artist awaits. All that's left to do now is to export your game level to the Web or as an EXE file, and you're done.

Time for action – who said you can't have your game and play it?

1. Before you do, walk around your level and check obvious things, such as the height of your eye level. If it's not quite right, use the **Scale** tool on your **First Person Controller** widget thing, as you can see below.

2. When that's done, make sure your level is saved (**File ¦ Save Scene**), and then go to **File ¦ Build and run**.

3. Select the following settings and add some graphics (Icon and splash screen image) if you have them (If you wish to export to web, select the Web Player platform instead).

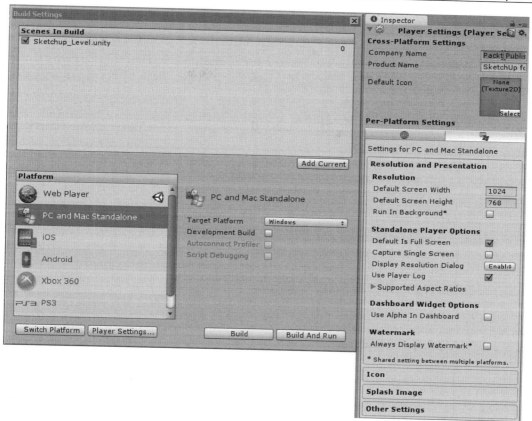

4. Click on **Build And Run**.

5. Type in your game file name and click on **Save**.

6. This time when you get the next screen, it's time to give yourself the full work. Select **Fantastic!**

Enjoy!

Summary

In this chapter, you took all your assets from SketchUp and made them into a walkthrough game. You learned how to set up your environment in Unity 3D. You learned how to create a realistic backdrop with an alpha map which you clipped in Unity to make parts of it see-through. You set up a skybox so that you could see clouds and sky above the buildings in the background and above you. There's been a lot to do in the chapter, but now you have a finished level. You can be proud of your achievement.

A
MakeHuman

Modeling people in 3D is just about the most difficult task you can undertake. It's best left to an expert in any case, and probably best done in another modeling package rather than SketchUp. But if despite this, you wish to have a go at making a human game asset in SketchUp, there's always MakeHuman, a human maker that's free to download. Isn't that convenient?

Time for action – making a human

1. Download and install the latest stable version of MakeHuman from `http://www.makehuman.org/`.

2. You also need MeshLab which we discovered in *Chapter 2, Tools that Grow on Trees*. We haven't done what we would have liked with MeshLab in this book because it's "work in progress" software and didn't produce stable and repeatable results. Let's have a look at it in the appendix, where it's safe to experiment!

3. When these are installed, start MakeHuman. You can experiment with all the settings to adjust Gender, Age, Muscle Tone, Weight, and Height. Those are the basics.

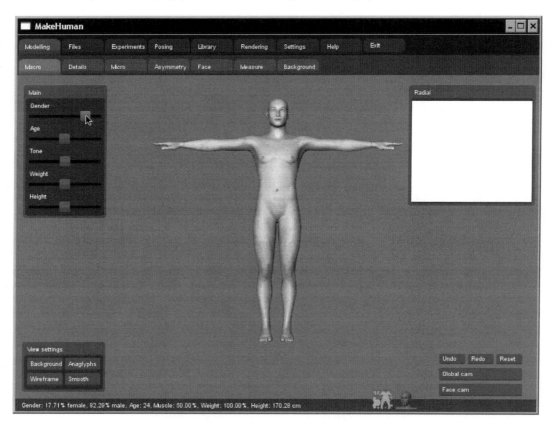

4. Now go to **Files ¦ Export** and deselect all the options. Select **Wavefront obj**.

5. Type in a filename and click on **Export**. That's all for now with MakeHuman.

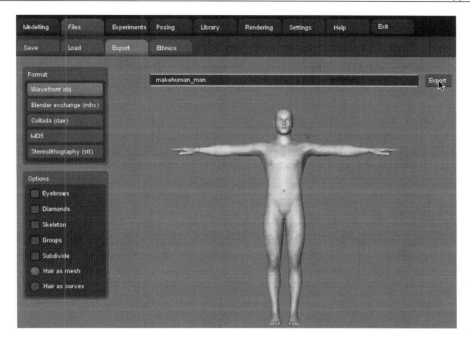

6. Go to Meshlab and open the file you just exported. You should find it in **My Documents | Makehuman |Exports** or something similar.

7. Here he is in MeshLab:

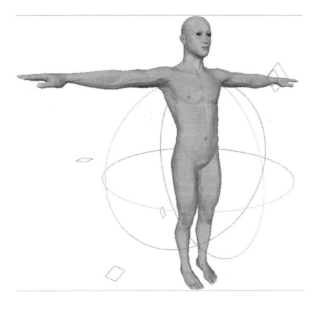

8. Did you notice how many polygons (faces) he's made up of? 27,500! That's way too many for game use.

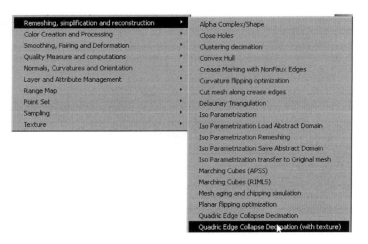

9. Go to **Quadratic Edge Collapse Decimation (with texture)** and try typing in **3000** faces. That should do it. Here he is now with the **Smooth view** button pressed:

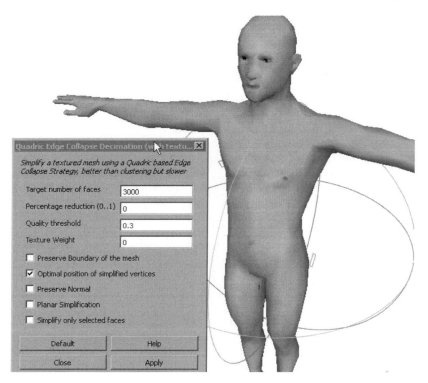

10. Go to **File ¦ Save As** and select **3DS format** and **Save**. Make sure you save him in the same folder as the texture.

11. In SketchUp, import the 3DS file. Here, he is:

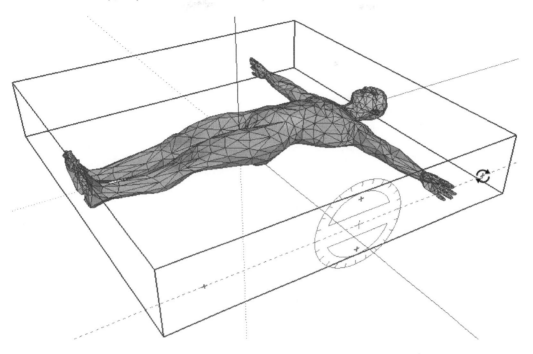

12. Turn him with the **Move** tool so that he's standing upright. Right-click and **Explode** once, and then use the **Soften/Smooth** tool.

What just happened?

You just made a textured, high-polygon human in MakeHuman, crunched the polygons down to a manageable level, and imported it into SketchUp. He is now there in all his low-polygon glory, texture and all. Here's a quick render in Shaderlight so you can see the realism even with vastly reduced polygons. You can now use him as a dressmaker's doll to help you model assets such as armor, weapons, or clothing, or work on him much in the same way as you did with the terrain and the car to create a game character or monster.

B
Pop Quiz Answers

Chapter 1: Why Use SketchUp

Question number	Answer
1	c
2	b

Chapter 2: Tools that Grow on Trees

Question number	Answer
1	Any three websites you have researched will do. If you don't know the answer, turn back to the *Have a go hero* exercise; research the game asset marketplace.
2	The answer here will be based on your own research.
3	Better viewed from a distance
4	A mesh
5	False

Chapter 6: Importing to a Professional Game Application: Unity 3D

Question number	Answer
1	The first person and the third person.
2	The outer extent to which the light will have an effect.
3	The *F* key
4	By ticking the **Generate colliders** box in the inspector when you import an asset. If you don't, your player character will fall through the floor, and keep falling.

Index

Symbols

2D map
creating 92
3D
human, modeling 241-246
3D assets
considerations, for creating 9
3D car outline
creating 178-181
3D game level 217
3D games 81
3D geometry
creating, for pallet 62-64
3D meshes, MeshLab 25-27
3D modelers
career, requisites 83, 84
3DS file 245
3D Warehouse
assets, researching 16-19
.xcf master file 175

A

advanced modeling
3D car outline, creating 178-181
car body filler, applying with pencil 187-189
car texture, creating 174-178
car texture, creating from photos 190
geometry, refining for car 181-186
Air Brush tool 227
alpha channel 146

B

ambient light
setting up, for buildings 236, 237
areas
fencing 148-151
filling, with textures 100-102
white edges, removing from 105-107
asset artist 83
asset modeler 83
asset modeling
textures, selecting for 39-42
assets
about 82, 159
researching 16-19
selling 11, 12
Autodesk FBX converter
using 122, 123
Auto White Balance filter 45

backdrop
creating 231, 232
background terrain
context, creating with 229
baking 217
basic 3D geometry, textures 58-61
blend areas
creating 199-201
blend layers
creating, from images 199
bonnet 181
Boolean tools 179

buildings
ambient light, setting up 236, 237
backdrop, creating 231, 232
creating 208-215
ee-through materials (Alpha Channel),
    enabling 233
exporting, to Unity 3D 227-229
fog effect, adding 235
gathering, between two images 153-155
generating, ultra quickly 153
interior, modeling 215-217
modular building block, making 156, 157
playable game level layout, setting up 218-222
see-through textures, creating 229-231
skybox, enabling 234
terrain, digging out 223-227
texturing, from photo materials 208-215

C

car
geometry, refining for 181-186
car body filler
applying, with pencil tool 187-189
car images
friend, finding on Flickr.com 192-196
locations, searching for 174
searching 191
taking 191
car parks 191
car's geometry
refining 181-186
car's geometry, refining
about 181
sitting, on bonnet 181-186
car texture
blend areas, creating 199-201
creating 174-178
creating, from photos 190
painting, in rear view 196-198
realistically wheels feature 204
URL 191
wheel, reinventing 189
car wheel
reinventing 189

CG texture
library 23
sources 20
URL 21
CGTextures.com
about 21, 39, 153
signing up for 21
Chain icon 193
character controller
game level, playing 133-136
setting up 132, 133
Circle tool 164, 189
Clone tool 210, 230
Colour Picker tool 199
colour selection layer
creating 92-94
component 62
context
creating, with background terrain 229
creating, with skyline 229
copyright issues, for textures 23
Cornucopia 12
Creative Commons attribution license 52
Crop Tool 43, 193

D

Drape tool
about 115
using 116

E

enhanced texture packs, Google 34, 36
Eraser Tool 145
Erase tool 184, 224

F

face alignment
verifying 162, 163
face orientation
verifying 78
FBX 28, 79
FBX Converter
URL, for downloading 28
FBX file 120

FBXImporter tab 134
features, SketchUp 9
fencing
    about 142
    making, with SketchUp's materials 142-144
    several unique variations, making 145, 146
    stuff, deforming for added realism 146
file formats, MeshLab 28
file formats, Unity 3D 28
Fill tool 199
first person shooter style controller
    setting up 132, 133
flat terrain
    height, adding to 107-110
Flickr.com 52
fog effect
    adding, to buildings 235
Fuzzy Select tool 104, 229

G

game asset marketplace
    researching 19, 20
game production
    parameters 83
games
    exporting 237-239
    temporary 3D Warehouse assets, using 227
game texture
    creating 43-45
geometry
    exploding 77
    refining, for car 181-186
GIMP
    about 36, 56, 93, 209
    URL, for installing 37
Google
    3D Warehouse 15, 16
    enhanced texture packs 34, 36
Google 3D Warehouse
    about 15
    assets, researching 16-19
    URL 16
Google Earth 8
Google SketchUp 15
Google Warehouse model
    cleaning up 159, 160

H

height
    adding, to flat terrain 107-110
hidden geometry
    about 26
    removing 160, 161
high-resolution terrain texture
    using, in Unity 3D 127, 128
human
    modeling 241-246

I

images
    blend layers, creating from 199
inference 63
instances 147, 229
interior
    modeling, for buildings 215-217
Internet
    tileable textures, using from 102

L

large areas
    fencing 148-151
large seamless texture
    creating 95-97
Layer Pallet 100
layers
    about 50
    naming 103
level
    about 81, 83
    creating 82
    exporting, from SketchUp 120, 121
level creation 82
level designer 83
lights
    creating 128
Line tool 58
locations
    searching, for car images 174
low polygon wrench
    modeling 166-171

M

MakeHuman
about 241
human, modeling 241-246
URL, for downloading 241
master texture
about 94
areas, filling with texture 100-102
large seamless texture, creating 95-97
multiples textures, combining in 52, 53
tiled texture, creating 98-100
materials
removing 77
Materials Pallet 68
Mesh 58
MeshLab
3D meshes 25-27
3D space 27
about 24, 26, 241
file formats 28
URL, for downloading 24
Middleware
about 28, 135
need for 29
modeling approach, SketchUp 56
model, preparing for game use
about 75
face orientation, verifying 78
geometry, exploding 77
hidden geometry 75
layers 75
materials, removing 77
textures, compressing 78, 79
textures, resizing 78, 79
unseen faces, removing 75-77
unused geometry, removing 77
Monochrome faces icon 78
Monochrome view 177
Move tool 63, 89, 96, 185, 211, 213
multiple textures
arranging 47-51
combining, in one master texture 52, 53

N

naming conventions, for texture 52

O

orbit tool 61
origin
fixing 160, 161
orthographic drawings 195, 196
orthographic views 175, 191
Outliner Pallet 76

P

Paint Brush tool 97
Paint Bucket tool 90, 143
pallet
3D geometry, creating for 62-64
copying, multiple times 137-140
pasting, multiple times 137-140
pencil tool
about 187
car body filler, applying with 187-189
Perspective tool 49, 194
photo
turning, into photo texture material 39-42
PhotoMatch tool 21
photo materials
building, texturing from 208-215
photos
car texture, creating from 190
Photoshop 36
photo texture
selecting 39-42
pixel 45
plate 82
playable game level layout
setting up 218-222
polygon 26
pre-prepared textures 67
pro games environment, Unity 3D 29
Push/Pull tool 62, 85, 213, 216

R

rear view image
painting 196-198
Rectangle tool 64, 216
roadside kerb
creating 103-105
Roofing Plates texture 212
Rotate tool 149

S

Sample function **74**
Sample Paint tool **211**
Sandbox tools
  terrain, modeling with **107**
scale issues
  rectifying **161**
Scale tool **192, 197**
seamless texture
  creating **95-97**
search feature
  using **174**
see-through materials (Alpha Channel)
  enabling **233**
see-through textures
  creating **229-231**
Select tool **65**
ShaderLight free version
  URL, for downloading **190**
sketching concept **84, 85**
SketchUp
  about **9**
  buildings, gathering between
      two images **153-155**
  buildings, generating ultra quickly **153**
  features **9**
  free Autodesk FBX converter, using **122, 123**
  get-up-and-get-started guide **56**
  hidden feature **65-67**
  level, exporting from **120, 121**
  limitations, for game asset modeling **10**
  modeling approach **56**
  model, preparing for export **120, 121**
  Move tool **63**
  multiple copies feature **65-67**
  multiple copies, inserting for
      filling out level **147**
  Push/Pull tool **62**
  Rectangle tool **64**
  sketching concept **84, 85**
  texture, importing **57, 58**
  textures, completing **68-72**
  textures, recycling **72-74**
  walking around, for visualizing levels **151, 152**
SketchUpColorPicker **68**
SketchUp free export **122**
SketchUp material
  fencing with **142-144**
SketchUp plugin
  URL **202**
SketchUp Pro **10, 122**
SketchUp Pro export **121**
skybox
  enabling **234**
skyline
  context, creating with **229**
Smoove tool **109**
Smudge tool **230**
sort selection box **17**
Stamp tool
  about **110**
  using **111-115**
Statistics option **68**
Sunlight
  creating, in Unity **129-132**

T

Tape Measure tool **175, 176, 211**
Targa format **54**
temporary 3D Warehouse assets
  using, in games **227**
ten-minute oil barrel **163-165**
terrain
  digging out **223-227**
  importing, to Unity 3D **123-127**
  modeling, with Sandbox tools **107**
terrain geometry
  merging, with texture **116**
terrain grid
  setting up **86-88**
terrain texture image
  setting up **89-91**
texture
  about **21**
  areas, filling with **100-102**
  basic 3D geometry **58-61**
  compressing **78, 79**
  copyright issues **23**
  copyright text **52**
  cropping **42-45**
  enhancing **42-45**
  importing, to scale **57, 58**

modeling from 58
multiple textures, arranging 47-51
naming conventions 52
pre-prepared textures 67
recycling 72-74
resizing 78, 79
saving 51
selecting, for using in asset modeling 39-42
size 46
terrain geometry, merging with 116, 117
texture library 23
texture maps 14
textures
verifying 162, 163
texture sizes 46
texturing
completing 68-72
Tgi3D SU Amorph Training Edition
URL 202
tileable textures
using, from Internet 102
tiled texture
creating 98-100
tiling 98
tools
modeling 166
tooltip 63
TurboSquid 191

U

Unity 3D
3D game level 217
about 8, 28
buildings, exporting to 227-229
high-resolution terrain texture,
    using in 127, 128
obtaining, for free 29-32
pro games environment 29
sunlight, creating in 129-132
terrain, importing to 123-127
URL, for downloading 29-32

Unity and Unity Pro licenses
URL, for differences 32
Unity sample assets
investigating 33, 34
Unity Tree creator
URL 233
unseen faces
removing 75-77
unused geometry
removing 77
UTV toolkit
URL 202
UV unwrap plugins
about 202
SketchUp 202
Tgi3D 202
using 203, 204
UTV toolkit 202

V

Vue 11
Vue users
online asset store 11

W

Wavefront object 242
white edges
removing, from areas of textures 105-107

Y

YouTube 15

Thank you for buying
Google SketchUp for Game Design:
Beginner's Guide

About Packt Publishing

Packt, pronounced 'packed', published its first book "Mastering phpMyAdmin for Effective MySQL Management" in April 2004 and subsequently continued to specialize in publishing highly focused books on specific technologies and solutions.

Our books and publications share the experiences of your fellow IT professionals in adapting and customizing today's systems, applications, and frameworks. Our solution-based books give you the knowledge and power to customize the software and technologies you're using to get the job done. Packt books are more specific and less general than the IT books you have seen in the past. Our unique business model allows us to bring you more focused information, giving you more of what you need to know, and less of what you don't.

Packt is a modern, yet unique publishing company, which focuses on producing quality, cutting-edge books for communities of developers, administrators, and newbies alike. For more information, please visit our website: www.PacktPub.com.

Writing for Packt

We welcome all inquiries from people who are interested in authoring. Book proposals should be sent to author@packtpub.com. If your book idea is still at an early stage and you would like to discuss it first before writing a formal book proposal, contact us; one of our commissioning editors will get in touch with you.

We're not just looking for published authors; if you have strong technical skills but no writing experience, our experienced editors can help you develop a writing career, or simply get some additional reward for your expertise.

SketchUp 7.1 for Architectural Visualization: Beginner's Guide

ISBN: 978-1-847199-46-1   Paperback:408 pages

Create stunning photo-realistic and artistic visuals for your SketchUp models

1. Create picture-perfect photo-realistic 3D architectural renders for your SketchUp models

2. Post-process SketchUp output to create digital watercolor and pencil art

3. Follow a professional visualization studio workflow

4. Make the most out of SketchUp with the best free plugins and add-on software to enhance your models

Unity 3D Game Development by Example Beginner's Guide

ISBN: 978-1-84969-054-6   Paperback: 384 pages

A seat-of-your-pants manual for building fun, groovy little games quickly

1. Build fun games using the free Unity 3D game engine even if you've never coded before

2. Learn how to "skin" projects to make totally different games from the same file – more games, less effort!

3. Deploy your games to the Internet so that your friends and family can play them

4. Packed with ideas, inspiration, and advice for your own game design and development

Please check **www.PacktPub.com** for information on our titles

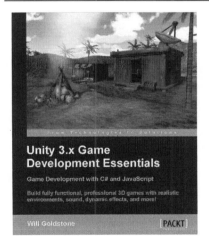